Charles Kingsley

Prose Idylls, New and Old

Charles Kingsley

Prose Idylls, New and Old

ISBN/EAN: 9783337370138

Printed in Europe, USA, Canada, Australia, Japan

Cover: Foto ©Thomas Meinert / pixelio.de

More available books at **www.hansebooks.com**

BY

REV. CHARLES KINGSLEY,

CANON OF WESTMINSTER.

FOURTH EDITION.

London:

MACMILLAN AND CO.

1878.

CONTENTS.

PROSE IDYLLS.

I.

'A CHARM OF BIRDS.'

B

PROSE IDYLLS.

1.

'*A CHARM OF BIRDS.*'[1]

Is it merely a fancy that we English, the educated people among us at least, are losing that love for spring which among our old forefathers rose almost to worship? That the perpetual miracle of the budding leaves and the returning song-birds awakes no longer in us the astonishment which it awoke yearly among the dwellers in the old world, when the sun was a god who was sick to death each winter, and returned in spring to life and health, and glory; when the death of Adonis, at the autumnal equinox, was wept over by the Syrian women, and the death of Baldur, in the colder north, by all living things, even to the dripping trees, and the rocks furrowed by the

[1] *Fraser's Magazine*, June 1867.

B 2

autumn rains; when Freya, the goddess of youth and love, went forth over the earth each spring, while the flowers broke forth under her tread over the brown moors, and the birds welcomed her with song; when, according to Olaus Magnus, the Goths and South Swedes had, on the return of spring, a mock battle between summer and winter, and welcomed the returning splendour of the sun with dancing and mutual feasting, rejoicing that a better season for fishing and hunting was approaching? To those simpler children of a simpler age, in more direct contact with the daily and yearly facts of Nature, and more dependent on them for their bodily food and life, winter and spring were the two great facts of existence; the symbols, the one of death, the other of life; and the battle between the two—the battle of the sun with darkness, of winter with spring, of death with life, of bereavement with love—lay at the root of all their myths and all their creeds. Surely a change has come over our fancies. The seasons are little to us now. We are nearly as comfortable in winter as in summer, or in spring. Nay, we have begun, of late, to grumble at the two latter as much as at the former, and talk (and not without excuse at times) of 'the treacherous month of May,' and of 'summer having set in with its usual severity.' We work for the most part in cities and towns, and the seasons pass by us unheeded. May and June are spent by most educated people anywhere rather than among birds and flowers. They do .not escape into the country till the elm hedges are growing black, and the song-birds silent, and the hay cut, and all the virgin bloom of the country has passed into a sober and matronly ripeness—if not into the sere and yellow leaf. Our very landscape painters, till Creswick arose and recalled to their minds the fact that trees were sometimes green, were wont to paint few but brown autumnal scenes. As for the song of birds, of which in the middle age no poet could say enough, our modern poets seem to be forgetting that birds ever sing.

It was not so of old. The climate, perhaps, was more severe than now; the transition from winter to spring more sudden, like that of Scandinavia now. Clearage of forests and drainage of land have equalized our seasons, or rather made them more uncertain. More broken winters are followed by more broken springs; and May-day is no longer a marked point to be kept as a festival by all childlike hearts. The merry month of May is merry only in stage songs. The May garlands and dances are all but gone: the borrowed plate, and the milkmaids who borrowed it, gone utterly. No more does Mrs. Pepys go to 'lie at Woolwich, in order to a little ayre and to gather

May-dew ' for her complexion, by Mrs. Turner's advice.
The Maypole is gone likewise; and never more shall
the puritan soul of a Stubbs be aroused in indigna-
tion at seeing 'against Maie, every parish, towne, and
village assemble themselves together, both men, women,
and children, olde and young, all indifferently, and
goe into the woodes and groves, hilles and mountaines,
where they spend the night in pastyme, and in the
morning they returne, bringing with them birch bowes
and braunches of trees to deck their assembly withal.
. . . They have twentie or fourtie yoke of oxen, every
oxe having a sweete nosegay of flowers tyed on the
tippe of his hornes, and these draw home this May-
pole (this stincking idol rather) which is covered all
over with flowers and hearbes, with two or three
hundred men, women, and children following it with
great devotion. . . . And then they fall to banquet
and feast, daunce and leap about it, as the heathen
people did at the dedication of their idolles, whereof
this is a perfect pattern, or the thing itself.'

This, and much more, says poor Stubbs, in his
' Anatomie of Abuses,' and had, no doubt, good reason
enough for his virtuous indignation at May-day scan-
dals. But people may be made dull without being
made good; and the direct and only effect of putting
down May games and such like was to cut off the
dwellers in towns from all healthy communion with

Nature, and leave them to mere sottishness and brutality.

Yet perhaps the May games died out, partly because the feelings which had given rise to them died out before improved personal comforts. Of old, men and women fared hardly, and slept cold; and were thankful to Almighty God for every beam of sunshine which roused them out of their long hybernation; thankful for every flower and every bird which reminded them that joy was stronger than sorrow, and life than death. With the spring came not only labour, but enjoyment:

> 'In the spring, the young man's fancy lightly turned to thoughts of love,'

as lads and lasses, who had been pining for each other by their winter firesides, met again, like Daphnis and Chloe, by shaugh and lea; and learnt to sing from the songs of birds, and to be faithful from their faithfulness.

Then went out troops of fair damsels to seek spring garlands in the forest, as Scheffel has lately sung once more in his 'Frau Aventiure;' and, while the dead leaves rattled beneath their feet, hymned 'La Regine Avrillouse' to the music of some Minnesinger, whose song was as the song of birds; to whom the birds were friends, fellow-lovers, teachers, mirrors of all

which he felt within himself of joyful and tender, true
and pure; friends to be fed hereafter (as Walther von
der Vogelweide had them fed) with crumbs upon his
grave.

True melody, it must be remembered, is unknown,
at least at present, in the tropics, and peculiar to the
races of those temperate climes, into which the song-
birds come in spring. It is hard to say why. Ex-
quisite songsters, and those, strangely, of an European
type, may be heard anywhere in tropical American
forests: but native races whose hearts their song
can touch, are either extinct or yet to come. Some
of the old German Minnelieder, on the other hand,
seem actually copied from the songs of birds. 'Tande-
radei' does not merely ask the nightingale to tell no
tales; it repeats, in its cadences, the nightingale's song,
as the old Minnesinger heard it when he nestled
beneath the lime-tree with his love. They are often
almost as inarticulate, these old singers, as the birds
from whom they copied their notes; the thinnest chain
of thought links together some bird-like refrain: but
they make up for their want of logic and reflection
by the depth of their passion, the perfectness of their
harmony with nature. The inspired Swabian, wan-
dering in the pine-forest, listens to the blackbird's
voice till it becomes his own voice; and he breaks
out, with the very carol of the blackbird—

' Vogele im Tannenwald pfeifet so hell.
Pfeifet de Wald aus und ein, wo wird mein Schätze sein ?
Vogele im Tannenwald pfeifet so hell.'

And he has nothing more to say. That is his whole soul for the time being; and, like a bird, he sings it over and over again, and never tires.

Another, a Nieder-Rheinischer, watches the moon rise over the Löwenburg, and thinks upon his love within the castle hall, till he breaks out in a strange, sad, tender melody—not without stateliness and manly confidence in himself and in his beloved—in the true strain of the nightingale :

'Verstohlen geht der Mond auf,
Blau, blau, Blümelein,
Durch Silberwölkchen führt sein Lauf.
Rosen im Thal, Mädel im Saal, O schönste Rosa !

. . . .

Und siehst du mich,
Und siehst du sie,
Blau, blau, Blümelein,
Zwei treu're Herzen sah'st du nie ;
Rosen im Thal u. s. w.'

There is little sense in the words, doubtless, according to our modern notions of poetry; but they are like enough to the long, plaintive notes of the nightingale to say all that the poet has to say, again and again through all his stanzas.

Thus the birds were, to the mediæval singers, their orchestra, or rather their chorus; from the birds they

caught their melodies; the sounds which the birds gave
them they rendered into words.

And the same bird key-note surely is to be traced in
the early English and Scotch songs and ballads, with
their often meaningless refrains, sung for the mere
pleasure of singing:

> 'Binnorie, O Binnorie.

Or—

> 'With a hey lillelu and a how lo lan,
> And the birk and the broom blooms bonnie.'

Or—

> ' 'She sat down below a thorn,
>   Fine flowers in the valley,
>   And there has she her sweet babe born,
>   And the green leaves they grow rarely.'

Or even those 'fal-la-las,' and other nonsense refrains,
which, if they were not meant to imitate bird-notes,
for what were they meant?

In the old ballads, too, one may hear the bird key-
note.   He who wrote (and a great rhymer he was)

> 'As I was walking all alane,
> I heard twa corbies making a mane,'

had surely the 'mane' of the 'corbies' in his ears
before it shaped itself into words in his mind: and he
had listened to many a 'woodwele' who first thrummed
on harp, or fiddled on crowd, how—

> ' In summer, when the shawes be shene,
>   And leaves be large and long,
>   It is full merry in fair forest
>   To hear the fowlés' song.
>
> ' The wood-wele sang, and wolde not cease,
>   Sitting upon the spray ;
>   So loud, it wakened Robin Hood
>   In the greenwood where he lay.'

And Shakespeare—are not his scraps of song
saturated with these same bird-notes ? ' Where the
bee sucks,' ' When daisies pied,' ' Under the green-
wood tree,' ' It was a lover and his lass,' ' When daf-
fodils begin to peer,' ' Ye spotted snakes,' have all a
ring in them which was caught not in the roar of
London, or the babble of the Globe theatre, but in
the woods of Charlecote, and along the banks of
Avon, from

> ' The ouzel-cock so black of hue,
>   With orange-tawny bill ;
>   The throstle with his note so true ;
>   The wren with little quill ;
>   The finch, the sparrow, and the lark,
>   The plain-song cuckoo gray'—

and all the rest of the birds of the air.

Why is it, again, that so few of our modern songs
are truly songful, and fit to be set to music ? Is it
not that the writers of them—persons often of much
taste and poetic imagination—have gone for their
inspiration to the intellect, rather than to the ear ?

That (as Shelley does by the skylark, and Words-
worth by the cuckoo), instead of trying to sing like
the birds, they only think and talk about the birds,
and therefore, however beautiful and true the thoughts
and words may be, they are not song? Surely they
have not, like the mediæval songsters, studied the
speech of the birds, the primæval teachers of melody;
nor even melodies already extant, round which, as
round a framework of pure music, their thoughts and
images might crystallize themselves, certain thereby
of becoming musical likewise. The best modern
song writers, Burns and Moore, were inspired by
their old national airs; and followed them, Moore
at least, with a reverent fidelity, which has had its
full reward. They wrote words to music; and not,
as modern poets are wont, wrote the words first, and
left others to set music to the words. They were
right; and we are wrong. As long as song is to
be the expression of pure emotion, so long it must
take its key from music,—which is already pure
emotion, untranslated into the grosser medium of
thought and speech—often (as in the case of Mendels-
sohn's Songs without Words) not to be translated into
it at all.

And so it may be, that in some simpler age, poets
may go back, like the old Minnesingers, to the birds of
the forest, and learn of them to sing.

And little do most of them know how much there is
to learn ; what variety of character, as well as variety
of emotion, may be distinguished by the practised ear,
in a 'charm of birds' (to use the old southern phrase),
from the wild cry of the missel-thrush, ringing from
afar in the first bright days of March, a passage of one
or two bars repeated three or four times, and then
another and another, clear and sweet, and yet defiant—
for the great 'stormcock' loves to sing when rain and
wind is coming on, and faces the elements as boldly as
he faces hawk and crow—down to the delicate warble
of the wren, who slips out of his hole in the brown
bank, where he has huddled through the frost with wife
and children, all folded in each other's arms like human
beings, for the sake of warmth,—which, alas ! does not
always suffice; for many a lump of wrens may be
found, frozen and shrivelled, after a severe winter.
Yet even he, sitting at his house-door in the low
sunlight, says grace for all mercies (as a little child
once worded it) in a song so rapid, so shrill, so loud,
and yet so delicately modulated, that you wonder at
the amount of soul within that tiny body ; and then
stops suddenly, as a child who has said its lesson, or
got to the end of the sermon, gives a self-satisfied flirt
of his tail, and goes in again to sleep.

Character ? I know not how much variety of cha-
racter there may be between birds of the same species :

but between species and species the variety is endless, and is shown—as I fondly believe—in the difference of their notes. Each has its own speech, inarticulate, expressing not thought but hereditary feeling ; save a few birds who, like those little dumb darlings, the spotted flycatchers, seem to have absolutely nothing to say, and accordingly have the wit to hold their tongues ; and devote the whole of their small intellect to sitting on the iron rails, flitting off them a yard or two to catch a butterfly in air, and flitting back with it to their nest.

But listen to the charm of birds in any sequestered woodland, on a bright forenoon in June. As you try to disentangle the medley of sounds, the first, perhaps, which will strike your ear will be the loud, harsh, monotonous, flippant song of the chaffinch ; and the metallic clinking of two or three sorts of titmice. But above the tree-tops, rising, hovering, sinking, the woodlark is fluting, tender and low. Above the pastures outside the skylark sings—as he alone can sing ; and close by, from the hollies rings out the blackbird's tenor—rollicking, audacious, humorous, all but articulate. From the tree above him rises the treble of the thrush, pure as the song of angels : more pure, perhaps, in tone, though neither so varied nor so rich, as the song of the nightingale. And there, in the next holly, is the nightingale himself : now croaking like a frog ; now talking aside to his wife

on the nest below; and now bursting out into that
song, or cycle of songs, in which if any man finds
sorrow, he himself surely finds none. All the morning
he will sing; and again at evening, till the small hours,
and the chill before the dawn: but if his voice sounds
melancholy at night, heard all alone, or only mocked
by the ambitious black-cap, it sounds in the bright
morning that which it is, the fulness of joy and love.
Milton's

> 'Sweet bird, that shun'st the noise of folly,
>   Most musical, most melancholy,'

is untrue to fact. So far from shunning the noise of
folly, the nightingale sings as boldly as anywhere close
to a stage-coach road, or a public path, as anyone will
testify who recollects the 'Wrangler's Walk' from
Cambridge to Trumpington forty years ago, when the
covert, which has now become hollow and shelterless,
held, at every twenty yards, an unabashed and jubilant
nightingale.

' Coleridge surely was not far wrong when he guessed
that—

> 'Some night-wandering man, whose heart was pierced
>   With the remembrance of a grievous wrong,
>   Or slow distemper, or neglected love
>   (And so, poor wretch, filled all things with himself,
>   And made all gentle sounds tell back the tale
>   Of his own sorrow)—he, and such as he,
>   First named these sounds a melancholy strain,
>   And many a poet echoes the conceit.'

That the old Greek poets were right, and had some grounds for the myth of Philomela, I do not dispute; though Sophocles, speaking of the nightingales of Colonos, certainly does not represent them as lamenting. The Elizabethan poets, however, when they talked of Philomel, 'her breast against a thorn,' were unaware that they and the Greeks were talking of two different birds; that our English Lusciola Luscinia is not Lusciola Philomela, one of the various birds called Bulbul in the East. The true Philomel hardly enters Venetia, hardly crosses the Swiss Alps, ventures not into the Rhine-land and Denmark, but penetrates (strangely enough) further into South Sweden than our own Luscinia: ranging meanwhile over all Central Europe, Persia, and the East, even to Egypt. Whether his song be really sad, let those who have heard him say. But as for our own Luscinia, who winters not in Egypt and Arabia, but in Morocco and Algeria, the only note of his which can be mistaken for sorrow, is rather one of too great joy; that cry, which is his highest feat of art; which he cannot utter when he first comes to our shores, but practises carefully, slowly, gradually, till he has it perfect by the beginning of June; that cry, long, repeated, loudening and sharpening in the intensity of rising passion, till it stops suddenly, exhausted at the point where pleasure, from very keenness, turns to pain; and—

' In the topmost height of joy
His passion clasps a secret grief.'

How different in character from his song is that of
the gallant little black-cap in the tree above him. A
gentleman he is of a most ancient house, perhaps the
oldest of European singing birds. How perfect must
have been the special organization which has spread,
seemingly without need of alteration or improvement,
from Norway to the Cape of Good Hope, from Japan
to the Azores. How many ages must have passed since
his forefathers first got their black caps. And how
intense and fruitful must have been the original
vitality which, after so many generations, can still fill
that little body with so strong a soul, and make him
sing as Milton's new-created birds sang to Milton's
Eve in Milton's Paradise. Sweet he is, and various,
rich, and strong, beyond all English warblers, save
the nightingale : but his speciality is his force, his
rush, his overflow, not so much of love as of happiness.
The spirit carries him away. He riots up and down
the gamut till he cannot stop himself; his notes
tumble over each other; he chuckles, laughs, shrieks
with delight, throws back his head, droops his tail, sets
up his back, and sings with every fibre of his body :
and yet he never forgets his good manners. He is
never coarse, never harsh, for a single note. Always

K

C

graceful, always sweet, he keeps perfect delicacy in his most utter carelessness.

And why should we overlook, common though he be, yon hedge-sparrow, who is singing so modestly, and yet so firmly and so true? Or cock-robin himself, who is here, as everywhere, honest, self-confident, and cheerful? Most people are not aware, one sometimes fancies, how fine a singer is cock-robin now in the spring-time, when his song is drowned by, or at least confounded with, a dozen other songs. We know him and love him best in winter, when he takes up (as he does sometimes in cold wet summer days) that sudden wistful warble, struggling to be happy, half in vain, which surely contradicts Coleridge's verse :—

'In Nature there is nothing melancholy.'

But he who will listen carefully to the robin's breeding song on a bright day in May, will agree, I think, that he is no mean musician; and that for force, variety and character of melody, he is surpassed only by black-cap, thrush, and nightingale.

And what is that song, sudden, loud, sweet, yet faltering, as if half ashamed? Is it the willow wren or the garden warbler? The two birds, though very remotely allied to each other, are so alike in voice, that it is often difficult to distinguish them, unless we attend carefully to the expression. For the garden

warbler, beginning in high and loud notes, runs down
in cadence, lower and softer, till joy seems conquered
by very weariness; while the willow wren, with a
sudden outbreak of cheerfulness, though not quite sure
(it is impossible to describe bird-songs without attri-
buting to the birds human passions and frailties) that
he is not doing a silly thing, struggles on to the end of
his story with a hesitating hilarity, in feeble imitation
of the black-cap's bacchanalian dactyls.

And now, again—is it true that

'In Nature there is nothing melancholy'?

Mark that slender, graceful, yellow warbler, running
along the high oak boughs like a perturbed spirit,
seeking restlessly, anxiously, something which he seems
never to find; and uttering every now and then a long
anxious cry, four or five times repeated, which would
be a squeal, were it not so sweet. Suddenly he flits
away, and flutters round the pendant tips of the beech-
sprays like a great yellow butterfly, picking the insects
from the leaves; then flits back to a bare bough, and
sings, with heaving breast and quivering wings, a short,
shrill, feeble, tremulous song; and then returns to his
old sadness, wandering and complaining all day long.
Is there no melancholy in that cry? It sounds sad:
why should it not be meant to be sad? We recognize
joyful notes, angry notes, fearful notes. They are very

similar (strangely enough) in all birds. They are very similar (more strangely still) to the cries of human beings, especially children, when influenced by the same passions. And when we hear a note which to us expresses sadness, why should not the bird be sad? Yon wood wren has had enough to make him sad, if only he recollects it; and if he can recollect his road from Morocco hither, he may be recollects likewise what happened on the road—the long weary journey up the Portuguese coast, and through the gap between the Pyrenees and the Jaysquivel, and up the Landes of Bordeaux, and across Brittany, flitting by night, and hiding and feeding as he could by day; and how his mates flew against the lighthouses, and were killed by hundreds; and how he essayed the British Channel, and was blown back, shrivelled up by bitter blasts; and how he felt, nevertheless, that 'that wan water he must cross,' he knew not why: but something told him that his mother had done it before him, and he was flesh of her flesh, life of her life, and had inherited her 'instinct'—as we call hereditary memory, in order to avoid the trouble of finding out what it is, and how it comes. A duty was laid on him to go back to the place where he was bred; and he must do it: and now it is done; and he is weary, and sad, and lonely; and, for aught we know, thinking already that when the leaves begin to turn yellow, he must go back again, over the Channel, over the Landes, over the Pyrenees, to Morocco once more. Why should he not be sad? He is a very delicate bird, as both his shape and his note testify. He can hardly keep up his race here in England; and is accordingly very uncommon, while his two cousins, the willow wren and the chiff-chaff, who, like him, build for some mysterious reason domed nests upon the ground, are stout, and busy, and numerous, and thriving everywhere. And what he has gone through may be too much for the poor wood wren's nerves; and he gives way; while willow wren, black-cap, nightingale, who have gone by the same road and suffered the same dangers, have stoutness of heart enough to throw off the past, and give themselves up to present pleasure. Why not?—who knows? There is labour, danger, bereavement, death in nature; and why should not some, at least, of the so-called dumb things know it, and grieve at it as well as we?

Why not?—Unless we yield to the assumption (for it is nothing more) that these birds act by some unknown thing called instinct, as it might be called x or y; and are, in fact, just like the singing birds which spring out of snuff-boxes, only so much better made, that they can eat, grow, and propagate their species. The imputation of acting by instinct cuts both ways. We, too, are creatures of instinct. We breathe and eat by instinct: but we talk and build houses by reason. And so may the birds. It is more philosophical, surely, to attribute actions in them to the same causes to which we attribute them (from experience) in ourselves. 'But if so,' some will say, 'birds must have souls.' We must define what our own souls are, before we can define what kind of soul or no-soul a bird may or may not have. The truth is, that we want to set up some 'dignity of human nature;' some innate superiority to the animals, on which we may pride ourselves as our own possession, and not return thanks with fear and trembling for it, as the special gift of Almighty God. So we have given the poor animals over to the mechanical philosophy, and allowed them to be considered as only mere cunningly devised pieces of watch-work, if philosophy would only spare us, and our fine human souls, of which we are so proud, though they are doing all the wrong and folly they can from one week's end to the other. And now our self-conceit has brought its own Nemesis; the mechanical philosophy is turning on us, and saying, 'The bird's "nature" and your "human nature" differ only in degree, but not in kind. If they are machines, so are you. They have no souls, you confess. You have none either.'

But there are those who neither yield to the mechanical philosophy nor desire to stifle it. While it is honest and industrious, as it is now, it can do nought but good, because it can do nought but discover facts.

It will only help to divide the light from the darkness,
truth from dreams, health from disease. Let it claim
for itself all that it can prove to be of the flesh, fleshly.
That which is spiritual will stand out more clearly
as of the Spirit. Let it thrust scalpel and microscope
into the most sacred penetralia of brain and nerve.
It will only find everywhere beneath brain and beneath
nerve, that substance and form which is not matter
nor phænomenon, but the Divine cause thereof; and
while it helps, with ruthless but wholesome severity,
to purge our minds from idols of the cave and idols of
the fane, it will leave untouched, more clearly defined,
and therefore more sacred and important than ever—

> ' Those first affections,
> Those shadowy recollections,
> Which, be they what they may,
> Are yet the fountain light of all our day,
> Are yet the master light of all our seeing ;
> Uphold us, cherish, and have power to make
> Our noisy years seem moments in the being
> Of the eternal silence ; truths that wake
> To perish never ;
> Which neither listlessness, nor mad endeavour,
> Nor man nor boy,
> Nor all that is at enmity with joy,
> Can utterly abolish or destroy.
> Then sing, ye birds, sing out with joyous sound,'

as the poet-philosopher bids you. Victorious analysis
will neither abolish you, nor the miraculous and un-

fathomable in you and in your song, which has stirred
the hearts of poets since first man was man. And if
anyone shall hint to us that we and the birds may have
sprung originally from the same type ; that the differ-
ence between our intellect and theirs is one of degree,
and not of kind, we may believe or doubt : but in either
case we shall not be greatly moved. ‘So much the
better for the birds,’ we will say, ‘and none the worse
for us. You raise the birds towards us: but you do
not lower us towards them. What we are, we are by
the grace of God. Our own powers and the burden
of them we know full well. It does not lessen their
dignity or their beauty in our eyes to hear that the
birds of the air partake, even a little, of the same gifts
of God as we. Of old said St. Guthlac in Crowland, as
the swallows sat upon his knee, “ He who leads his life
according to the will of God, to him the wild deer and
the wild birds draw more near; ” and this new theory
of yours may prove St. Guthlac right. St. Francis, too
—he called the birds his brothers. Whether he was
correct, either theologically or zoologically, he was
plainly free from that fear of being mistaken for an ape,
which haunts so many in these modern times. Per-
fectly sure that he himself was a spiritual being, he
thought it at least possible that birds might be spiritual
beings likewise, incarnate like himself in mortal flesh ;
and saw no degradation to the dignity of human nature

in claiming kindred lovingly with creatures so beautiful, so wonderful, who (as he fancied in his old-fashioned way) praised God in the forest, even as angels did in heaven. In a word, the saint, though he was an ascetic, and certainly no man of science, was yet a poet, and somewhat of a philosopher; and would have possibly—so do extremes meet—have hailed as orthodox, while we hail as truly scientific, Wordsworth's great saying—

> ' Therefore am I still
> A lover of the meadows and the woods
> And mountains ; and of all that we behold
> From this green earth ; of all the mighty world
> Of eye and ear—both what they half create,
> And what perceive ; well pleased to recognize
> In Nature and the language of the sense,
> The anchor of my purest thoughts, the nurse,
> The guide, the guardian of my heart, and soul
> Of all my moral being.'

II.

CHALK-STREAM STUDIES.

CHALK-STREAM STUDIES.[1]

FISHING is generally associated in men's minds with wild mountain scenery; if not with the alps and cataracts of Norway, still with the moors and lochs of Scotland, or at least with the rocky rivers, the wooded crags, the crumbling abbeys of Yorkshire, Derbyshire, Hereford, or the Lowlands. And it cannot be denied that much of the charm which angling exercises over cultivated minds, is due to the beauty and novelty of the landscapes which surround him; to the sense of freedom, the exhilarating upland air. Who would prefer the certainty of taking trout out of some sluggish preserve, to the chance of a brace out of Edno or Llyn Dulyn? The pleasure lies not in the prize itself, but in the pains which it has cost; in the upward climbs through the dark plantations, beside the rock-walled stream; the tramp over the upland pastures, one gay

[1] *Fraser's Magazine*, September 1858.

flower-bed of blue and purple butter-wort; the steady breathless climb up the crags, which looked but one mile from you when you started, so clear against the sky stood out every knoll and slab; the first stars of the white saxifrage, golden-eyed, blood-bedropt, as if a fairy had pricked her finger in the cup, which shine upon some green cushion of wet moss, in a dripping crack of the cliff; the first grey tufts of the Alpine club-moss, the first shrub of crowberry, or sea-green rose-root, with its strange fleshy stems and leaves, which mark the two-thousand-feet-line, and the beginning of the Alpine world; the scramble over the arid waves of the porphyry sea aloft, as you beat round and round like a weary pointer dog in search of the hidden lake; the last despairing crawl to the summit of the Syenite pyramid on Moel Meirch; the hasty gaze around, far away into the green vale of Ffestiniog, and over wooded flats, and long silver river-reaches, and yellow sands, and blue sea flecked with flying clouds, and isles and capes, and wildernesses of mountain peaks. east. west. south, and north; one glance at the purple gulf out of which Snowdon rises, thence only seen in full majesty from base to peak: and then the joyful run, springing over bank and boulder, to the sad tarn beneath your feet: the loosening of the limbs, as you toss yourself, bathed in perspiration, on the turf; the almost awed pause as you recollect that you are alone on the mountain-tops, by the side of the desolate pool, out of all hope of speech or help of man; and, if you break your leg among those rocks, may lie there till the ravens pick your bones; the anxious glance round the lake to see if the fish are moving; the still more anxious glance through your book to guess what they will choose to take; what extravagant bundle of red, blue, and yellow feathers, like no insect save perhaps some jewelled monster from Amboyna or Brazil—may tempt those sulkiest and most capricious of trout to cease for once their life-long business of picking leeches from among those Syenite cubes which will twist your ankles and break your shins for the next three hours. What matter (to a minute philosopher, at least) if, after two hours of such enjoyment as that, he goes down again into the world of man with empty creel, or with a dozen pounders and two-pounders, shorter, gamer, and redder-fleshed than ever came out of Thames or Kennet? What matter? If he has not caught them, he might have caught them; he has been catching them in imagination all the way up; and if he be a minute philosopher, he holds that there is no falser proverb than that devil's beatitude—'Blessed is he who expecteth nothing, for he shall not be disappointed.'

Say, rather, Blessed is he who expecteth everything, for he enjoys everything once at least: and if it falls out true, twice also.

Yes. Pleasant enough is mountain fishing. But there is one objection against it, that it is hard work to get to it; and that the angler, often enough half-tired before he arrives at his stream or lake, has left for his day's work only the lees of his nervous energy.

Another objection, more important perhaps to a minute philosopher than to the multitude, is, that there is in mountain-fishing an element of excitement: an element which is wholesome enough at times for every one; most wholesome at all times for the man pent up in London air and London work; but which takes away from the angler's most delicate enjoyment, that dreamy contemplative repose, broken by just enough amusement to keep his body active, while his mind is quietly taking in every sight and sound of nature. Let the Londoner have his six weeks every year among crag and heather, and return with lungs expanded and muscles braced to his nine months' prison. The countryman, who needs no such change of air and scene, will prefer more home-like, though more homely, pleasures. Dearer than wild cataracts or Alpine glens are the still hidden streams which Bewick has immortalized in his vignettes, and Creswick in his pictures; the long glassy shallow, paved with yellow gravel, where he wades up between low walls of fern-fringed rock, beneath nut, and oak. and alder, to the low bar over which the stream comes swirling and dimpling, as the water-ouzel flits piping before him, and the murmur of the ringdove comes soft and sleepy through the wood. There, as he wades, he sees a hundred sights and hears a hundred tones, which are hidden from the traveller on the dusty highway above. The traveller fancies that he has seen the country. So he has; the outside of it, at least: but the angler only sees the inside. The angler only is brought close face to face with the flower, and bird, and insect life of the rich river banks, the only part of the landscape where the hand of man has never interfered, and the only part in general which never feels the drought of summer, ' the trees planted by the waterside whose leaf shall not wither.'

Pleasant are those hidden waterways: but yet are they the more pleasant because the hand of man has not interfered with them ?

It is a question, and one which the older one grows the less one is inclined to answer in the affirmative. The older one grows, the more there grows on one the sense of waste and incompleteness in all scenery where man has not fulfilled the commission of Eden, ' to dress it and to keep it;' and with that, a sense of loneliness which makes one long for home, and cultivation, and the speech of fellow men.

Surely the influence of mountain scenery is exagge-rated now-a-days. In spite of the reverend name of Wordsworth (whose poetry, be it remembered, too often

K   D

wants that element of hardihood and manliness which is supposed to be the birthright of mountaineers), one cannot help, as a lowlander, hoping that there is a little truth in the threnodes of a certain peevish friend who literally hates a mountain, and justifies his hatred in this fashion :—

'I do hate mountains. I would not live among them for ten thousand a year. If they look like paradise for three months in the summer, they are a veritable inferno for the other nine; and I should like to condemn my mountain-worshipping friends to pass a whole year under the shadow of Snowdon, with that great black head of his shutting out the sunlight, staring down into their garden, overlooking all they do in the most impertinent way, sneezing and spitting at them with rain, hail, snow, and bitter freezing blasts, even in the hottest sunshine. A mountain? He is a great stupid giant, with a perpetual cold in his head, whose highest ambition is to give you one also. As for his beauty, no natural object has so little of its own; he owes it to the earthquakes that reared him up, to the rains and storms which have furrowed him, to every gleam and cloud which pass over him. In himself he is a mere helpless stone-heap. Our old Scandinavian forefathers were right when they held the mountain Yotuns to be helpless pudding-headed giants, the sport of gods and men: and their English descendant, in spite of all his second-hand sentiment, holds the same opinion at his heart ; for his first instinct, jolly honest fellow that he is, on seeing a snow alp, is to scramble up it and smoke his cigar upon the top. And this great stupid braggart, pretending to be a personage and an entity, which, like Pope's monument on Fish-street hill,

"Like a tall bully, lifts the head and lies,"

I am called upon now-a-days to worship, as my better, my teacher. Shall I, the son of Odin and Thor, worship Hrymir the frost giant, and his cows the water-falls ? Shall I bow down to the stock of a stone ? My better ? I have done an honest thing or two in my life, but I never saw a mountain do one yet. As for his superiority to me, in what does it consist ? His strength ? If he be stronger than I, let him cut stones out of my ribs, as I can out of his. His size ? Am I to respect a mountain the more for being 10,000 feet high ? As well ask me to respect Daniel Lambert for weighing five-and-twenty stone. His cunning con-struction ? There is not a child which plays at his foot, not an insect which basks on his crags, which is not more fearfully and wonderfully made ; while as for his grandeur of form, any college youth who scrambles up him, peel him out of his shooting jacket and trousers, is a hundred times more beautiful, and more grand too,

by all laws of art. But so it is. In our prurient pru-
dery, we have got to despise the human, and therefore
the truly divine, element in art, and look for inspira-
tion, not to living men and women, but to leaves and
straws, stocks and stones. It is an idolatry baser than
that of the old Canaanites ; for they had the courage
to go up to the mountain tops, and thence worship
the host of heaven: but we are to stay at the bottom,
and worship the mountains themselves. Byron began
the folly with his misanthropic "Childe Harold."
Sermons in stones? I don't believe in them. I have
seen a better sermon in an old peasant woman's face
than in all the Alps and Apennines of Europe. Did
you ever see any one who was the better for moun-
tains? Have the Alps made * * * a whit honester,
or * * * a whit more good-natured, or Lady * * * a
whit cleverer? Do they alter one hair's breadth for
the better the characters of the ten thousand male and
female noodles who travel forth to stare at them every
year? Do mountains make them lofty-minded and
generous-hearted? No. Cælum, non animum mutant,
qui trans mare currunt. Don't talk to me of the moral
and physical superiority of mountain races, for I tell
you it is a dream. Civilization, art, poetry, belong to
the lowlands. Are the English mountaineers, pray, or
the French, or the Germans? Were the Egyptians
mountaineers, or the Romans, or the Assyrians, as soon

as they became a people? The Greeks lived among
mountains, but they took care to inhabit the plains;
and it was the sea and not the hills which made them
the people which they were. Does Scotland owe her
life to the highlander, or to the lowlander? If you
want an experimentum crucis, there is one. As for
poetry, will you mention to me one mountain race
which has written great poetry? You will quote the
Hebrews. I answer that the life of Palestine always
kept to the comparatively low lands to the west of
Jordan, while the barbarous mountaineers of the eastern
range never did anything,—had but one Elijah to show
among them. Shakspeare never saw a hill higher
than Malvern Beacon; and yet I suppose you will
call him a poet? Mountaineers look well enough
at a distance; seen close at hand you find their
chief distinctions to be starvation and ignorance, fleas
and goitre, with an utter unconsciousness—unless
travellers put it into their heads—of the "soul-ele-
vating glories" by which they have been surrounded
all their lives.'

He was gently reminded of the existence of the
Tyrolese.

'You may just as wisely remind me of the Circas-
sians. What can prove my theory more completely
than the fact that in them you have the two finest
races of the world, utterly unable to do anything for

humanity, utterly unable to develop themselves, because, to their eternal misfortune, they have got caged among those abominable stoneheaps, and have not yet been able to escape ? '

It was suggested that if mountain races were generally inferior ones, it was because they were the remnants of conquered tribes driven up into the highlands by invaders.

'And what does that prove but that the stronger and cunninger races instinctively seize the lowlands, because they half know (and Providence knows altogether) that there alone they can become nations, and fulfil the primæval mission—to replenish the earth and subdue it ? No, no, my good sir. Mountains are very well when they are doing their only duty—that of making rain and soil for the lowlands : but as for this new-fangled admiration of them, it is a proof that our senses are dulled by luxury and books, and that we require to excite our palled organ of marvellousness by signs and wonders, æsthetic brandy and cayenne. No. I have remarked often that the most unimaginative people, who can see no beauty in a cultivated English field or in the features of a new-born babe, are the loudest ravers about glorious sunsets and Alpine panoramas : just as the man with no music in his soul, to whom a fugue of Sebastian Bach, or one of Mendelssohn's Songs without Words, means nothing, and is nothing thinks a monster concert of drums and trumpets un-commonly fine.'

This is certainly a sufficiently one-sided diatribe. Still it is one-sided : and we have heard so much of the other side of late, that it may be worth while to give this side also a fair and patient hearing.

At least he who writes wishes that it may have a fair hearing. He has a sort of sympathy with Lord Macaulay's traveller of a hundred and fifty years since, who amid the 'horrible desolation' of the Scotch highlands, sighs for 'the true mountain scenery of Richmond-hill.' The most beautiful landscape he has ever seen, or cares to see, is the vale of Thames from Taplow or from Cliefden, looking down towards Wind-sor, and up toward Reading; to him Bramshill, looking out far and wide over the rich lowland from its eyrie of dark pines, or Littlecote nestling between deer-spotted upland and rich water-meadow, is a finer sight than any robber castle of the Rhine. He would not complain, of course, were either of the views backed, like those glorious ones of Turin or Venice, by the white saw-edge of the distant Alps : but chiefly because the perpetual sight of that Alp-wall would increase the sense of home, of guarded security, which not the mountain, but the sea, or the very thought of the sea, gives to all true Englishmen.

Let others therefore (to come back to angling) tell

of moor and loch. But let it be always remembered
that the men who have told of them best have not been
mountaineers, but lowlanders who carried up to the
mountain the taste and knowledge which they had
gained below. Let them remember that the great
Sutherlandshire sportsman and sporting writer, the
late Mr. St. John, was once a fine gentleman about
town; that Christopher North was an Edinburgh Pro-
fessor, a man of city learning and city cultivation; and,
as one more plea for our cockney chalk-streams of
the south, that Mr. Scrope (who passed many pleasant
years respected and beloved by Kennet side, with
Purdy at his heels) enjoyed, they say, the killing of
a Littlecote trout as heartily as he did that of a
Tweed salmon.

Come, then, you who want pleasant fishing-days
without the waste of time and trouble and expense
involved in two hundred miles of railway journey,
and perhaps fifty more of highland road; and try what
you can see and do among the fish not sixty miles from
town. Come to pleasant country inns, where you can
always get a good dinner; or, better still, to pleasant
country houses, where you can always get good society;
to rivers which will always fish, brimfull in the longest
droughts of summer, instead of being, as those mountain
ones are, very like a turnpike-road for three weeks, and
then like bottled porter for three days; to streams on

which you have strong south-west breezes for a week together on a clear fishing water, instead of having, as on those mountain ones, foul rain spate as long as the wind is south-west, and clearing water when the wind chops up to the north, and the chill blast of 'Clarus Aquilo' sends all the fish shivering to the bottom ; streams, in a word, where you may kill fish (and large ones) four days out of five from April to October, instead of having, as you will most probably in the mountain, just one day's sport in the whole of your month's holiday. Deluded friend, who suffered in Scotland last year a month of Tantalus his torments, furnished by art and nature with rods, flies, whisky, scenery, keepers, salmon innumerable, and all that man can want, except water to fish in ; and who returned, having hooked accidentally by the tail one salmon—which broke all and ween to sea—why did you not stay at home and take your two-pounders and three-pounders out of the quiet chalk brook which never sank an inch through all that drought, so deep in the caverns of the hills are hidden its mysterious wells ? Truly, wise men bide at home, with George Riddler, while 'a fool's eyes are in the ends of the earth.'

Repent, then ; and come with me, at least in fancy, at six o'clock upon some breezy morning in June, not by roaring railway nor by smoking steamer, but in the cosy four-wheel, along brown heather moors, down into green clay woodlands, over white chalk downs, past Roman camps and scattered blocks of Sarsden stone, till we descend into the long green vale where, among groves of poplar and abele, winds silver Whit. Come and breakfast at the neat white inn, of yore a posting-house of fame. The stables are now turned into cottages ; and instead of a dozen spruce ostlers and helpers, the last of the postboys totters sadly about the yard and looks up eagerly at the rare sight of a horse to feed. But the house keeps up enough of its ancient virtue to give us a breakfast worthy of Pantagruel's self ; and after it, while we are looking out our flies, you can go and chat with the old postboy, and hear his tales, told with a sort of chivalrous pride, of the noble lords and fair ladies before whom he has ridden in the good old times gone by—even, so he darkly hints, before ' His Royal Highness the Prince ' himself. Poor old fellow, he recollects not, and he need not recollect, that these great posting-houses were centres of corruption, from whence the newest vices of the metropolis were poured into the too-willing ears of village lads and lasses ; and that not even the New Poor Law itself has done more for the morality of the South of England than the substitution of the rail for coaches.

Now we will walk down through the meadows some half mile.

While all the land in flowery squares,
Beneath a broad and equal-blowing wind
Smells of the coming summer,'

to a scene which, as we may find its antitype any-
where for miles round, we may boldly invent for our-
selves.

A red brick mill (not new red brick, of course) shall
hum for ever below giant poplar-spires, which bend
and shiver in the steady breeze. On its lawn labur-
nums shall feather down like dropping wells of gold,
and from under them the stream shall hurry leaping
and laughing into the light, and spread at our feet into
a broad bright shallow, in which the kine are standing
knee-deep already: a hint, alas! that the day means
heat. And there, to the initiated eye, is another and
a darker hint of glaring skies, perspiring limbs, and
empty creels. Small fish are dimpling in the central
eddies: but here, in six inches of water, on the very
edge of the ford road, great tails and back-fins are
showing above the surface, and swirling suddenly
among the tufts of grass, sure sign that the large fish
are picking up a minnow-breakfast at the same time
that they warm their backs, and do not mean to look at
a fly for many an hour to come.

Yet courage; for on the rail of yonder wooden bridge
sits, chatting with a sun-browned nymph, her bonnet
pushed over her face, her hayrake in her hand, a river-

god in coat of velveteen, elbow on knee and pipe in mouth, who, rising when he sees us, lifts his wide-awake, and halloas back a roar of comfort to our mystic adjuration,—

'Keeper! Is the fly up?'

'Mortial strong last night, gentlemen.'

Wherewith he shall lounge up to us, landing-net in hand, and we will wander up stream and away.

We will wander—for though the sun be bright, here are good fish to be picked out of sharps and stop-holes —into the water-tables, ridged up centuries since into furrows forty feet broad and five feet high, over which the crystal water sparkles among the roots of the rich grass, and hurries down innumerable drains to find its parent stream between tufts of great blue geranium, and spires of purple loosestrife, and the delicate white and pink comfrey-bells, and the avens—fairest and most modest of all the water-side nymphs, who hangs her head all day long in pretty shame, with a soft blush upon her tawny cheek. But at the mouth of each of those drains, if we can get our flies in, and keep ourselves unseen, we will have one cast at least. For at each of them, in some sharp-rippling spot, lies a great trout or two, waiting for beetle, caterpillar, and whatsoever else may be washed from among the long grass above. Thence, and from brimming feeders, which slip along, weed-choked, under white hawthorn hedges, and beneath the great roots of oak and elm, shall we pick out full many a goodly trout. There, in yon stop-hole underneath that tree, not ten feet broad or twenty long, where just enough water trickles through the hatches to make a ripple, are a brace of noble fish, no doubt ; and one of them you may be sure of, if you will go the proper way to work, and fish scientifically with the brace of flies I have put on for you—a governor and a black alder. In the first place, you must throw up into the little pool, not down. If you throw down, they will see you in an instant; and besides, you will never get your fly close under the shade of the brick-work, where alone you have a chance. What use in throwing into the still shallow tail, shining like oil in the full glare of the sun ?

'But I cannot get below the pool without——'

Without crawling through that stiff stubbed hedge, well set with trees, and leaping that ten-foot feeder afterwards. Very well. It is this sort of thing which makes the stay-at-home cultivated chalk-fishing as much harder work than mountain angling, as a gallop over a stiffly enclosed country is harder than one over an open moor. You can do it or not, as you like : but if you wish to catch large trout on a bright day, I should advise you to employ the only method yet discovered.

There—you are through ; and the keeper shall hand

you your rod. You have torn your trousers, and got a couple of thorns in your shins. The one can be mended, the other pulled out. Now, jump the feeder. There is no run to it, so—you have jumped in. Never mind: but keep the point of your rod up. You are at least saved the lingering torture of getting wet inch by inch; and as for cold water hurting any one—Credat Judæus.

Now make a circuit through the meadow forty yards away. Stoop down when you are on the ridge of each table. A trout may be basking at the lower end of the pool, who will see you, rush up, and tell all his neighbours. Take off that absurd black chimney-pot, which you are wearing, I suppose, for the same reason as Homer's heroes wore their koruthous and phalerous, to make yourself look taller and more terrible to your foes. Crawl up on three legs; and when you are in position, kneel down. So.

Shorten your line all you can—you cannot fish with too short a line up-stream; and throw, not into the oil-basin near you, but right up into the darkest corner. Make your fly strike the brickwork and drop in.— So? No rise? Then don't work or draw it, or your deceit is discovered instantly. Lift it out, and repeat the throw.

What? You have hooked your fly in the hatches? Very good. Pull at it till the casting-line breaks; put on a fresh one, and to work again. There! you have him. Don't rise! fight him kneeling; hold him hard, and give him no line, but shorten up anyhow. Tear and haul him down to you before he can make to his home, while the keeper runs round with the net. . . . . There, he is on shore. Two pounds, good weight. Creep back more cautiously than ever, and try again. . . . . . There. A second fish, over a pound weight. Now we will go and recover the flies off the hatches; and you will agree that there is more cunning, more science, and therefore more pleasant excitement, in 'foxing' a great fish out of a stop-hole, than in whipping far and wide over an open stream, where a half-pounder is a wonder and a triumph. As for physical exertion, you will be able to compute for yourself how much your back, knees, and fore-arm will ache by nine o'clock to-night, after some ten hours of this scrambling, splashing, leaping, and kneeling upon a hot June day. This item in the day's work will of course be put to the side of loss or of gain, according to your temperament: but it will cure you of an inclination to laugh at us Wessex chalk-fishers as Cockneys.

So we will wander up the streams, taking a fish here and a fish there, till——Really it is very hot. We have the whole day before us; the fly will not be up till five o'clock at least; and then the real fishing will begin. Why tire ourselves beforehand? The squire will send us luncheon in the afternoon, and after that expect us to fish as long as we can see, and come up to the hall to sleep, regardless of the ceremony of dressing. For is not the green drake on? And while he reigns, all hours, meals, decencies, and respectabilities must yield to his caprice. See, here he sits, or rather tens of thousands of him, one on each stalk of grass— green drake, yellow drake, brown drake, white drake, each with his gauzy wings folded over his back, waiting for some unknown change of temperature, or something else, in the afternoon, to wake him from his sleep, and send him fluttering over the stream; while overhead the black drake, who has changed his skin and reproduced his species, dances in the sunshine, empty, hard, and happy, like Festus Bailey's Great Black Crow, who all his life sings 'Ho, ho, ho,'

'For no one will eat him,'he well doth know.'

However, as we have insides, and he has actually none, and what is more strange, not even a mouth wherewith to fill the said insides, we had better copy his brothers and sisters below whose insides are still left, and settle with them upon the grass awhile beneath yon goodly elm.

Comfort yourself with a glass of sherry and a biscuit, and give the keeper one, and likewise a cigar. He will value it at five times its worth, not merely for the pleasure of it, but because it raises him in the social scale. ' Any cad,' so he holds, ' smokes pipes ; but a good cigar is the mark of the quality,' and of them who ' keep company with the quality,' as keepers do. He puts it in his hat-crown, to smoke this evening in presence of his compeers at the public-house, retires modestly ten yards, lies down on his back in a dry feeder, under the shade of the long grass, and instantly falls fast asleep. Poor fellow ! he was up all last night in the covers, and will be again to-night. Let him sleep while he may, and we will chat over chalk-fishing.

The first thing, probably, on which you will be inclined to ask questions, is the size of the fish in these streams. We have killed this morning four fish averaging a pound weight each. All below that weight we throw in, as is our rule here ; but you may have remarked that none of them exceeded half a pound; that they were almost all about herring size. The smaller ones I believe to be year-old fish, hatched last spring twelvemonth ; the pound fish two-year-olds. At what rate these last would have increased depends very much, I suspect, on their chance of food. The limit of life and growth in cold-blooded animals seems to depend very much on their amount of food. The boa, alligator, shark, pike, and I suppose the trout also, will live to a great age, and attain an enormous size, give them but range enough; and the only cause why there are trout of ten pounds and more in the Thames lashers, while one of four pounds is rare here, is simply that the Thames fish has more to eat. Here, were the fish not sufficiently thinned out every year by anglers, they would soon become large-headed, brown, and flabby, and cease to grow. Many a good stream has been spoilt in this way, when a squire has unwisely preferred quantity to quality of fish.

And if it be not the quantity of feed, I know no clear reason why chalk and limestone trout should be so much larger and better flavoured than any others. The cause is not the greater swiftness of the streams; for (paradoxical as it may seem to many) a trout likes swift water no more than a pike does, except when spawning or cleaning afterwards. At those times his blood seems to require a very rapid oxygenation, and he goes to the 'sharps' to obtain it: but when he is feeding and fattening, the water cannot be too still for him. Streams which are rapid throughout never produce large fish; and a hand-long trout transferred from his native torrent to a still pond, will increase in size at a ten times faster rate. In chalk streams the largest fish are found oftener in the mill-heads than in the mill tails. It is a mistake, though a common one, to fancy that the giant trout of the Thames lashers lie in swift water. On the contrary, they lie in the very stillest spot of the whole pool, which is just under the hatches. There the rush of the water shoots over their heads, and they look up through it for every eatable which may be swept down. At night they run down to the fan of the pool, to hunt minnow round the shallows; but their home by day is the still deep; and their preference of the lasher pool to the quiet water above is due merely to the greater abundance of food. Chalk trout, then, are large not merely because the water is swift.

Whether trout have not a specific fondness for lime; whether water of some dozen degrees of hardness is not necessary for their development? are questions which may be fairly asked. Yet is not the true reason this; that the soil on the banks of a chalk or limestone stream is almost always rich—red loam, carrying an abundant vegetation, and therefore an abundant crop of animal life, both in and out of the water? The countless insects which haunt a rich hay meadow, all know who have eyes to see; and if they will look into the stream they will find that the water-world is even richer than the air-world.

Every still spot in a chalk stream becomes so choked with weed as to require moving at least thrice a year, to supply the mills with water. Grass, milfoil, water crowfoot, hornwort, starwort, horsetail, and a dozen other delicate plants, form one tangled forest, denser than those of the Amazon, and more densely peopled likewise.

To this list will soon be added our Transatlantic curse, *Babingtonia diabolica*, alias *Anacharis alsinastrum*. It has already ascended the Thames as high as Reading; and a few years more, owing to the present aqua-vivarium mania, will see it filling every mill-head in England, to the torment of all millers. Young ladies are assured that the only plant for their vivariums is a sprig of anacharis, for which they pay sixpence— the market value being that of a wasp, flea, or other scourge of the human race; and when the vivarium fails, its contents, Anacharis and all, are tost into the nearest ditch; for which the said young lady ought to be fined five pounds; and would be, if Governments governed. What an 'if'

But come; for the sun burns bright, and fishing is impossible: lie down upon the bank, above this stop. There is a campshutting (a boarding in English) on which you can put your elbows. Lie down on your face, and look down through two or three feet of water clear as air into the water forest where the great trout feed.

Here; look into this opening in the milfoil and crowfoot bed. Do you see a grey film around that sprig? Examine it through the pocket lens. It is a forest of glass bells, on branching stalks. They are Vorticellæ; and every one of those bells, by the ciliary current on its rim, is scavenging the water—till a tadpole comes by and scavenges it. How many millions of living creatures are there on that one sprig? Look here!—a brown polype, with long waving arms—a gigantic monster, actually a full half-inch long. He is *Hydra fusca,* most famous, and earliest described (I think by Trembley). Ere we go home I may show you perhaps *Hydra viridis,* with long pea-green arms; and *rosca,* most beautiful in form and colour of all the strange family. You see that lump, just where his stalk joins his bell-head? That is a budding baby. Ignorant of the joys and cares of wedlock, he increases by gemmation. See! here is another, with a full-sized young one growing on his back. You may tear it off if you will—he cares not. You may cut him into a dozen pieces, they say, and each one will grow, as a potato does. I suppose, however, that he also sends out of his mouth little free ova—medusoids— call them what you will, swimming by ciliæ, which afterwards, unless the water beetles stop them on the way, will settle down as stalked polypes, and in their turn practise some mystery of Owenian parthenogenesis, or Steenstruppian alternation of generations, in which all traditional distinctions of plant and animal, male and female, are laughed to scorn by the magnificent fecundity of the Divine imaginations.

That dusty cloud which shakes off in the water as you move the weed, under the microscope would be one mass of exquisite forms—Desmidiæ and Diatomaceæ, and what not? Instead of running over long names, take home a little in a bottle, put it under your microscope, and if you think good verify the species from Hassall, Ehrenberg, or other wise book; but without doing that, one glance through the lens will show you why the chalk trout grow fat.

Do they, then, eat these infusoria?

That is not clear. But minnows and small fry eat them by millions; and so do tadpoles, and perhaps caddis baits and water crickets.

What are they?

Look on the soft muddy bottom. You see numberless bits of stick. Watch awhile, and those sticks are alive, crawling and tumbling over each other. The weed, too, is full of smaller ones. Those live sticks are the larva-cases of the Caperers—Phryganeæ—of which one family nearly two hundred species have been already found in Great Britain. Fish up one, and you find, amid sticks and pebbles, a comfortable silk case, tenanted by a goodly grub. Six legs he has, like all insects, and tufts of white horns on each ring of his abdomen, which are his gills. A goodly pair of jaws

he has too, and does good service with them: for he
is the great water scavenger. Decaying vegetable
matter is his food, and with those jaws he will bark a
dead stick as neatly as you will with a penknife. But
he does not refuse animal matter. A dead brother
(his, not yours) makes a savoury meal for him; and
a party of those Vorticellæ would stand a poor chance
if he came across them. You may count these caddis
baits by hundreds of thousands; whether the trout eat
them case and all, is a question in these streams. In
some rivers the trout do so; and what is curious, during
the spring, have a regular gizzard, a temporary thick-
ening of the coats of the stomach, to enable them to
grind the pebbly cases of the caddises. See! here is
one whose house is closed at both ends—'grillé,' as
Pictet calls it, in his unrivalled monograph of the
Genevese Phryganeæ, on which he spent four years of
untiring labour. The grub has stopped the mouth of
his case by an open network of silk, defended by small
pebbles, through which the water may pass freely,
while he changes into his nymph state. Open the
case; you find within not a grub, but a strange bird-
beaked creature, with long legs and horns laid flat by
its sides, and miniature wings on its back. Observe
that the sides of the tail, and one pair of legs, are
fringed with dark hairs. After a fortnight's rest in
this prison this 'nymph' will gnaw her way out and

swim through the water on her back, by means of that
fringed tail and paddles, till she reaches the bank and
the upper air. There, under the genial light of day,
her skin will burst, and a four-winged fly emerge, to
buzz over the water as a fawn-coloured Caperer—dead-
liest of trout flies; if she be not snapped up beforehand
under water by some spotted monarch in search of
supper.

But look again among this tangled mass of weed.
Here are more larvæ of water-flies. Some have the
sides fringed with what look like paddles, but are
gills. Of these one part have whisks at the tail, and
swim freely. They will change into ephemeræ, cock-
winged 'duns,' with long whisked tails. The larvæ of the
famous green drake (*Ephemera vulgata*) are like these:
but we shall not find them. They are all changed by
now into the perfect fly; and if not, they burrow about
the banks, and haunt the crayfish-holes, and are not
easily found.

Some, again, have the gills on their sides larger and
broader, and no whisks at the tail. These are the larvæ
of Sialis, the black alder, Lord Stowell's fly, shorm fly,
hunch-back of the Welsh, with which we have caught
our best fish to-day.

And here is one of a delicate yellow-green, whose
tail is furnished with three broad paddle-blades. These,
I believe, are gills again. The larva is probably that

of the Yellow Sally—*Chrysoperla viridis*—a famous fly on hot days in May and June. Among the pebbles there, below the fall, we should have found, a month since, a similar but much larger grub, with two paddles at his tail. He is the 'creeper' of the northern streams, and changes to the great crawling stone fly (May-fly of Tweed), *Perla bicaudata*, an ugly creature, which runs on stones and posts, and kills right well on stormy days, when he is beaten into the stream.

There. Now we have the larvæ of the four great trout-fly families, Phryganeæ, Ephemeræ, Sialidæ, Perlidæ; so you have no excuse for telling—as not only Cockneys, but really good sportsmen who write on fishing, have done — such fibs as that the green drake comes out of a caddis-bait, or giving such vague generalities as, 'this fly comes from a water-larva.'

These are, surely, in their imperfect and perfect states, food enough to fatten many a good trout : but they are not all. See these transparent brown snails, Limneæ and Succinæ, climbing about the posts ; and these other pretty ones, coil laid within coil as flat as a shilling, Planorbis. Many a million of these do the trout pick off the weed day by day; and no food, not even the leech, which swarms here, is more fattening. The finest trout of the high Snowdon lakes feed almost entirely on leech and snail—baits they have none—and fatten till they cut as red as a salmon.

Look here too, once more. You see a grey moving cloud about that pebble bed, and underneath that bank. It is a countless swarm of 'sug,' or water-shrimp ; a bad food, but devoured greedily by the great trout in certain overstocked preserves.

Add to these plenty of minnow, stone-loach, and miller's thumbs, a second course of young crayfish, and for one gormandizing week of bliss, thousands of the great green-drake fly : and you have food enough for a stock of trout which surprise, by their size and number, an angler fresh from the mountain districts of the north and west. To such a fisherman, the tale of Mr. * * *, of Ramsbury, who is said to have killed in one day in his own streams on Kennet, seventy-six trout, all above a pound, sounds like a traveller's imagination: yet the fact is, I believe, accurately true.

This, however, is an extraordinary case upon an extraordinary stream. In general, if a man shall bring home (beside small fish) a couple of brace of from one to three pounds apiece, he may consider himself as a happy man, and that the heavens have not shone, but frowned, upon him very propitiously.

And now comes another and an important question. For which of all these dainty eatables, if for any, do the trout take our flies? and from that arises another. Why are the flies with which we have been fishing this morning so large—of the size which is usually employed on a Scotch lake? You are a North-country fisher, and are wont, upon your clear streams, to fish with nothing but the smallest gnats. And yet our streams are as clear as yours: what can be clearer?

Whether fish really mistake our artificial flies for different species of natural ones, as Englishmen hold; or merely for something good to eat, the colour whereof strikes their fancy, as Scotchmen think—a theory which has been stated in detail, and with great semblance of truth, in Mr. Stewart's admirable 'Practical Angler,'—is a matter about which much good sense has been written on both sides.

Whosoever will, may find the great controversy fully discussed in the pages of Ephemera. Perhaps (as in most cases) the truth lies between the two extremes; at least, in a chalk-stream.

Ephemera's list of flies may be very excellent, but it is about ten times as long as would be required for any of our southern streams. Six or seven sort of flies ought to suffice for any fisherman; if they will not kill, the thing which will kill is yet to seek.

To name them:—

1. The caperer.
2. The March-brown.

3. The governor.

4. The black alder.

And two or three large palmers, red, grizzled, and coch-a-bonddhu, each with a tuft of red floss silk at the tail. These are enough to show sport from March to October; and also like enough to certain natural flies to satisfy the somewhat dull memory of a trout.

But beyond this list there is little use in roaming, as far as my experience goes. A yellow dun kills sometimes marvellously on chalk-streams, and always upon rocky ones. A Turkey-brown ephemera, the wing made of the bright brown tail of the cock partridge, will, even just after the May-fly is off, show good sport in the forenoon, when he is on the water; and so will in the evening the claret spinner, to which he turns. Excellent patterns of these flies may be found in Ronalds: but, after all, they are uncertain flies; and, as Harry Verney used to say, ' they casualty flies be all havers;' which sentence the reader, if he understands good Wessex, can doubtless translate for himself.

And there are evenings on which the fish take greedily small transparent ephemerae. But, did you ever see large fish rise at these ephemerae? And even if you did, can you imitate the natural fly? And after all, would it not be waste of time? For the experience of many good fishers is, that trout rise at these delicate duns, black gnats, and other microscopic trash, simply *faute de mieux.* They are hungry, as trout are six days in the week, just at sunset. A supper they must have, and they take what comes; but if you can give them anything better than the minute fairy, compact of equal parts of glass and wind, which naturalists call an Ephemera or Bætis, it will be most thankfully received, if there be ripple enough on the water (which there seldom is on a fine evening) to hide the line: and even though the water be still, take boldly your caperer or your white moth (either of them ten times as large as what the trout are rising at), hurl it boldly into a likely place, and let it lie quiet and sink, not attempting to draw or work it; and if you do not catch anything by that means, comfort yourself with the thought that there are others who can.

And now to go through our list, beginning with—

1. The caperer.

This perhaps is the best of all flies; it is certainly the one which will kill earliest and latest in the year; and though I would hardly go as far as a friend of mine, who boasts of never fishing with anything else, I believe it will, from March to October, take more trout, and possibly more grayling, than any other fly. Its basis is the woodcock wing; red hackle legs, which should be long and pale; and a thin mohair body, of different shades of red-brown, from a dark claret to a pale sandy. It may thus, tied of different sizes, do duty for half-a-dozen of the commonest flies; for the early claret (red-brown of Ronalds; a Nemoura, according to him), which is the first spring-fly; for the red spinner, or perfect form of the March-brown ephemera; for the soldier, the soft-winged reddish beetle which haunts the umbelliferous flowers, and being as soft in spirit as in flesh, perpetually falls into the water, and comes to grief therein; and last but not least, for the true caperers, or whole tribe of Phryganidæ, of which a sketch was given just now. As a copy of them, the body should be of a pale red brown, all but sandy (but never snuff-coloured, as shop-girls often tie it), and its best hour is always in the evening. It kills well when fish are gorged with their morning meal of green drakes; and after the green drake is off, it is almost the only fly at which large trout care to look; a fact not to be wondered at when one considers that nearly two hundred species of English Phryganidæ have been already described, and that at least half of them are of the fawn-tint of the caperer. Under the title of flame-brown, cinnamon, or red-hackle and rail's wing, a similar fly kills well in Ireland, and in Scotland also; and is sometimes the best sea-trout fly which can be laid on the water. Let this suffice for the caperer.

2. Of the March-brown ephemera there is little to be said, save to notice Ronalds' and Ephemera's excel-

lent description, and Ephemera's good hint of fishing with more than one March-brown at once, viz. with a sandy-bodied male, and a greenish-bodied female. The fly is a worthy fly, and being easily imitated, gives great sport, in number rather than in size; for when the March-brown is out, the two or three pound fish are seldom on the move, preferring leeches, tom-toddies, and caddis-bait in the nether deeps, to slim ephemeræ at the top; and if you should (as you may) get hold of a big fish on the fly, 'you'd best hit him in again,' as we say in Wessex; for he will be, like the Ancient Mariner—

'Long, and lank, and brown,
As is the ribbed sea-sand.'

3. The 'governor.'—In most sandy banks, and dry poor lawns, will be found numberless burrows of ground bees who have a great trick of tumbling into the water. Perhaps, like the honey bee, they are thirsty souls, and must needs go down to the river and drink; perhaps, like the honey bee, they rise into the air with some difficulty, and so in crossing a stream are apt to strike the further bank, and fall in. Be that as it may, an imitation of these little ground bees is a deadly fly the whole year round; and if worked within six inches of the shore, will sometimes fill a basket when there is not a fly on the water or a fish rising. There are those who never put up a cast of flies without one; and

those, too, who have killed large salmon on him in the north of Scotland, when the streams are low.

His tie is simple enough. A pale partridge or woodcock wing, short red hackle legs, a peacock-herl body, and a tail—on which too much artistic skill can hardly be expended—of yellow floss silk, and gold twist or tinsel. The orange-tailed governors ' of ye shops,' as the old drug-books would say, are all ' havers;' for the proper colour is a honey yellow. The mystery of this all-conquering tail seems to be, that it represents the yellow pollen, or ' bee bread' in the thighs or abdomen of the bee; whereof the bright colour, and perhaps the strong musky flavour, makes him an attractive and savoury morsel. Be that as it may, there is no better rule for a chalk stream than this—when you don't know what to fish with, try the governor.

4. The black alder (*Sialis nigra*, or *Lutaria*).

What shall be said, or not be said, of this queen of flies ? And what of Ephemera, who never mentions her ? His alder fly is—I know not what; certainly not that black alder, shorm fly, Lord Stowell's fly, or hunchback, which kills the monsters of the deep, surpassed only by the green drake for one fortnight; but surpassing him in this, that she will kill on till September, from that happy day on which

> ' You find her out on every stalk
> Whene'er you take a river walk,
> When swifts at eve begin to hawk.'

O thou beloved member of the brute creation! Songs have been written in praise of thee; statues would ere now have been erected to thee, had that hunch back and those flabby wings of thine been 'susceptible of artistic treatment.' But ugly thou art in the eyes of the uninitiated vulgar; a little stumpy old maid toddling about the world in a black bonnet and a brown cloak, laughed at by naughty boys, but doing good wherever thou comest, and leaving sweet memories behind thee; so sweet that the trout will rise at the ghost or sham of thee, for pure love of thy past kindnesses to them, months after thou hast departed from this sublunary sphere. What hours of bliss do I not owe to thee! How have I seen, in the rich meads of Wey, after picking out wretched quarter-pounders all the morning on March-brown and red-hackle, the great trout rush from every hover to welcome thy first appearance among the sedges and buttercups! How often, late in August, on Thames, on Test, on Loddon heads, have I seen the three and four pound fish prefer thy dead image to any live reality. Have I not seen poor old Si. Wilder, king of Thames fishermen (now gone home to his rest), shaking his huge sides with delight over thy mighty deeds, as his fourteen-inch whiskers fluttered in the breeze like the horse-tail standard of some great Bashaw, while crystal Thames murmured over the white flints on Monkey Island shallow, and

K   F

the soft breeze sighed in the colossal poplar spires, and the great trout rose and rose, and would not cease, at thee, my alder-fly? Have I not seen, after a day in which the earth below was iron, and the heavens above as brass, as the three-pounders would have thee, and thee alone, in the purple August dusk, old Moody's red face grow redder with excitement, half proud at having advised me to 'put on' thee, half fearful lest we should catch all my lady's pet trout in one evening? Beloved alder-fly! would that I could give thee a soul (if indeed thou hast not one already, thou, and all things which live), and make thee happy in all æons to come! But as it is, such immortality as I can I bestow on thee here, in small return for all the pleasant days thou hast bestowed on me.

Bah! I am becoming poetical; let us think how to tie an alder-fly.

The common tie is good enough. A brown mallard, or dark hen-pheasant tail for wing, a black hackle for legs, and the necessary peacock-herl body. A better still is that of Jones Jones Beddgelert, the famous fishing clerk of Snowdonia, who makes the wing of dappled peacock-hen, and puts the black hackle on before the wings, in order to give the peculiar hunch-backed shape of the natural fly. Many a good fish has this tie killed. But the best pattern of all is tied from the mottled wing-feather of an Indian bustard; generally used, when it can be obtained, only for salmon flies. The brown and fawn check pattern of this feather seems to be peculiarly tempting to trout, especially to the large trout of Thames; and in every river where I have tried the alder, I have found the bustard wing *facile princeps* among all patterns of the fly.

Of palmers (the hairy caterpillars) are many sorts. Ephemera gives by far the best list yet published. Ronalds has also three good ones, but whether they are really taken by trout instead of the particular natural insects which he mentions, is not very certain. The little coch-a-bonddhu palmer, so killing upon moor streams, may probably be taken for young larvæ of the fox and oak-egger moths, abundant on all moors, upon trefoils, and other common plants; but the lowland caterpillars are so abundant and so various in colour that trout must be good entomologists to distinguish them. Some distinction they certainly make; for one palmer will kill where another does not: but this depends a good deal on the colour of the water; the red palmer, being easily seen, will kill almost anywhere and any when, simply because it is easily seen; and both the grizzle and brown palmer may be made to kill by adding to the tail a tuft of red floss silk; for red, it would seem, has the same exciting effect on fish which it has upon many quadrupeds, possibly because it is the colour of flesh. The mackerel will often run greedily

at a strip of scarlet cloth; and the most killing pike-fly
I ever used had a body made of remnants of the hunts-
man's new 'pink.' Still, there are local palmers. On
Thames, for instance, I have seldom failed with the
grizzled palmer, while the brown has seldom succeeded,
and the usually infallible red never. There is one more
palmer worth trying, which Scotsmen, I believe, call the
Royal Charlie; a coch-a-bonddhu or furnace hackle, over
a body of gold-coloured floss silk, ribbed with broad gold
tinsel. Both in Devonshire and in Hampshire this will
kill great quantities of fish, wherever furzy or otherwise
wild banks or oak-woods afford food for the oak-egger
and fox moths, which children call 'Devil's Gold Rings,'
and Scotsmen 'Hairy Oubits.'

Two hints more about palmers. They must not be
worked on the top of the water, but used as stretchers,
and allowed to sink as living caterpillars do; and next,
they can hardly be too large or rough, provided that
you have skill enough to get them into the water with-
out a splash. I have killed well on Thames with one
full three inches long, armed of course with two small
hooks. With palmers—and perhaps with all baits—
the rule is, the bigger the bait the bigger the fish. A
large fish does not care to move except for a good
mouthful. The best pike-fisher I know prefers a half-
pound chub when he goes after one of his fifteen-pound
jack; and the largest pike I ever ran—and lost, alas!—

who seemed of any weight above twenty pounds, was hooked on a live white fish of full three-quarters of a pound. Still, no good angler will despise the minute North-country flies. In Yorkshire they are said to kill the large chalk trout of Driffield as well as the small limestone and grit fish of Craven; if so, the gentlemen of the Driffield Club, who are said to think nothing of killing three-pound fish on midge flies and cobweb tackle, must be (as canny Yorkshiremen are likely enough to be) the best anglers in England.

In one spot only in Yorkshire, as far as I know, do our large chalk flies kill: namely, in the lofty limestone tarn of Malham. There palmers, caperers, and rough black flies, of the largest Thames and Kennet sizes, seem the only attractive baits: and for this reason, that they are the flies of the place. The cinnamon Phryganea comes up abundantly from among the stones; and the large peat moss to the west of the tarn abounds, as usual, in house-flies and bluebottles, and in the caterpillars of the fox and oak-egger moths: another proof that the most attractive flies are imitations of the real insects. On the other hand, there are said to be times when midges, and nothing else, will rise fish on some chalk streams. The delicate black hackle which Mr. Stewart praises so highly (and which should always be tied on a square sneck-bend hook) will kill in June and July; and on the Itchen, at Winchester, hardly any

flies but small ones are used after the green drake is off.
But there is one sad objection against these said midges
—what becomes of your fish when hooked on one in
a stream full of weeds (as all chalk streams are after
June), save

> 'One struggle more, and I am free
> From pangs which rend my heart in twain '?

Winchester fishers have confessed to me that they
lose three good fish out of every four in such cases;
and as it seems pretty clear that chalk fish approve
of no medium between very large flies and very small
ones, I advise the young angler, whose temper is not
yet schooled into perfect resignation, to spare his own
feelings by fishing with a single large fly—say the
governor in the forenoon, the caperer in the evening,
regardless of the clearness of the water. I have seen
flies large enough for April, raise fish excellently in
Test and other clear streams in July and August; and,
what is more, drag them up out of the weeds and into
the landing-net, where midges would have lost them in
the first scuffle.

So much for our leading chalk flies; all copies
of live insects. Of the entomology of mountain
streams little as yet is known: but a few scattered
hints may suffice to show that in them, as well as in
the chalk rivers, a little natural science might help
the angler.

The well-known fact that smaller flies are required on the moors than in the lowlands, is easily explained by the fact that poorer soils and swifter streams produce smaller insects. The large Phryganeæ, or true caperers, whose caddis-baits love still pools and stagnant ditches, are there rare; and the office of water-scavenger is fulfilled by the Rhyacophiles (torrent-lovers) and Hydropsyches, whose tiny pebble-houses are fixed to the stones to resist the violence of the summer floods. In and out of them the tiny larva runs to find food, making in addition, in some species, galleries of earth along the surface of the stones, in which he takes his walks abroad in full security. In any of the brown rivulets of Windsor forest, towards the middle of summer, the pebble-houses of these little creatures may be seen in millions, studding every stone. To the Hydropsyches (species *montana?* or *variegata?* of Pictet) belongs that curious little Welsh fly, known in Snowdon by the name of the Gwynnant, whose tesselated wing is best imitated by brown mallard feather, and who so swarms in the lower lakes of Snowdon, that it is often necessary to use three of them on the line at once, all other flies being useless. It is perhaps the abundance of these tesselated Hydropsyches which makes the mallard wing the most useful in mountain districts, as the abundance of the fawn and grey Phryganidæ in the south of England makes the woodcock wing justly the favourite.

The Rhyacophiles, on the other hand, are mostly of a shining soot-grey, or almost black. These may be seen buzzing in hundreds over the pools on a wet evening, and with them the sooty Mystacides, called silver-horns in Scotland, from their antennæ, which are of preposterous length, and ringed prettily enough with black and white. These delicate fairies make moveable cases, or rather pipes, of the finest sand, generally curved, and resembling in shape the Dentalium shell. Guarded by these, they hang in myriads on the smooth ledges of rock, where the water runs gently a few inches deep. These are abundant everywhere: but I never saw so many of them as in the exquisite Cother brook, near Middleham, in Yorkshire. In that delicious glen, while wading up beneath the ash-fringed crags of limestone, out of which the great ring ouzel (too wild, it seemed, to be afraid of man) hopped down fearlessly to feed upon the strand, or past flower-banks where the golden globe-flower, and the great blue geranium, and the giant campanula bloomed beneath the white tassels of the bird-cherry, I could not tread upon the limestone slabs without crushing at every step hundreds of the delicate Mystacide tubes, which literally paved the shallow edge of the stream, and which would have been metamorphosed in due time into small sooty moth-like fairies, best represented, I should say, by the soft black-hackle which Mr. Stewart recommends as the most deadly of North-country flies. Not to these, however, but to the Phryganeæ (who, when sticks and pebbles fail, often make their tubes of sand, e. g. *P. flava*), should I refer the red-cow fly, which is almost the only autumn killer in the Dartmoor streams. A red cow-hair body and a woodcock wing is his type, and let those who want West-country trout remember him.

Another fly, common on some rocky streams, but more scarce in the chalk, is the 'Yellow Sally,' which entomologists, with truer appreciation of its colour, call *Chrysoperla viridis.* It may be bought at the shops; at least a yellow something of that name, but bearing no more resemblance to the delicate yellow-green natural fly, with its warm grey wings, than a Pre-Raphaelite portrait to the human being for whom it is meant. Copied, like most trout flies, from some tra-ditional copy by the hands of Cockney maidens, who never saw a fly in their lives, the mistake of a mistake, a sham raised to its tenth power, it stands a signal proof that anglers will never get good flies till they learn a little entomology themselves, and then teach it to the tackle makers. But if it cannot be bought, it can at least be made; and I should advise every-one who fishes rocky streams in May and June, to dye for himself some hackles of a brilliant greenish-yellow, and in the most burning sunshine, when fish seem inclined to rise at no fly whatsoever, examine the boulders for the Chrysoperla, who runs over them, her wings laid flat on her back, her yellow legs moving as rapidly as a forest-fly's; try to imitate her, and use her on the stream, or on the nearest lake. Certain it is that in Snowdon this fly and the Gwynnant Hydropsyche will fill a creel in the most burning north-easter, when all other flies are useless; a sufficient disproof of the Scotch theory—that fish do not prefer the fly which is on the water.[1]

Another disproof may be found in the 'fern web,' 'bracken clock' of Scotland; the tiny cockchafer, with brown wing-cases and dark-green thorax, which abounds in some years in the hay-meadows, on the fern, or on the heads of umbelliferous flowers. The famous Loch-Awe fly, described as an alder-fly with a rail's wing, seems to be nothing but this fat little worthy : but the best plan is to make the wings, either buzz or hackle, of the bright neck-feather of the cock pheasant, thus gaining the metallic lustre of the beetle tribe. Tied thus, either in Devonshire or Snowdon, few flies surpass him when he is out. His fatness proves an attraction which the largest fish cannot resist.

The Ephemeræ, too, are far more important in

---

[1] The Ripon list of natural flies contains several other species of small Nemouridæ unknown to me, save one brown one, which is seen in the South, though rarely, in June.

rapid and rocky streams than in the deeper, stiller
waters of the south. It is worth while for a good
fish to rise at them there; the more luxurious chalk
trout will seldom waste himself upon them, unless he
be lying in shallow water, and has but to move a few
inches upward.

But these Ephemeræ, like all other naiads, want
working out. The species which Mr. Ronalds gives,
are most of them, by his own confession, very uncertain.
Of the Phryganidæ he seems to know little or nothing,
mentioning but two species out of the two hundred
which are said to inhabit Britain; and his land flies and
beetles are in several cases quite wrongly named. How-
ever, the professed entomologists know but little of the
mountain flies; and the angler who would help to work
them out would confer a benefit on science, as well as
on the 'gentle craft.' As yet the only approach to
such a good work which I know of, is a little book on
the trout flies of Ripon, with excellent engravings of
the natural fly. The author's name is not given; but
the book may be got at Ripon, and most valuable it
must be to any North-country fisherman.

But come, we must not waste our time in talk, for
here is a cloud over the sun, and plenty more coming
up behind, before a ruffling south-west breeze, as Shelley
has it—

'Calling white clouds like flocks to feed in air.'

Let us up and onward to that long still reach, which is now curling up fast before the breeze; there are large fish to be taken, one or two at least, even before the fly comes on. You need not change your flies; the cast which you have on—governor, and black alder—will take, if anything will. Only do not waste your time and muscle, as you are beginning to do, by hurling your flies wildly into the middle of the stream, on the chance of a fish being there. Fish are there, no doubt, but not feeding ones. They are sailing about and enjoying the warmth; but nothing more. If you want to find the hungry fish and to kill them, you must stand well back from the bank—or kneel down, if you are really in earnest about sport; and throw within a foot of the shore, above you or below (but if possible above), with a line short enough to manage easily; by which I mean short enough to enable you to lift your flies out of the water at each throw without hooking them in the docks and comfrey which grow along the brink. You must learn to raise your hand at the end of each throw, and lift the flies clean over the land-weeds: or you will lose time, and frighten all the fish, by crawling to the bank to unhook them. Believe me, one of the commonest mistakes into which young anglers fall is that of fishing in 'skip-jack broad;' in plain English, in mid-stream, where few fish, and those little ones, are to be caught. Those

who wish for large fish work close under the banks, and
seldom take a mid-stream cast, unless they see a fish
rise there.

The reason of this is simple. Walking up the
Strand in search of a dinner, a reasonable man will
keep to the trottoir, and look in at the windows close
to him, instead of parading up the mid-street. And
even so do all wise and ancient trout. The banks
are their shops; and thither they go for their dinners,
driving their poor little children tyrannously out into
the mid-river to fare as hap may hap. Over these
children the tyro wastes his time, flogging the stream
across and across for weary hours, while the big papas
and mammas are comfortably under the bank, close at
his feet, grubbing about the sides for water crickets,
and not refusing at times a leech or a young crayfish,
but perfectly ready to take a fly if you offer one large
and tempting enough. They do but act on experience.
All the largest surface-food—beetles, bees, and palmers
—comes off the shore; and all the caperers and alders,
after emerging from their pupa-cases, swim to the
shore in order to change into the perfect insect in the
open air. The perfect insects haunt sunny sedges and
tree-stems—whence the one is often called the sedge,
the other the alder-fly—and from thence drop into the
trouts' mouths; and within six inches of the bank
will the good angler work, all the more sedulously and

even hopefully if he sees no fish rising. I have known good men say that they had rather *not* see fish on the rise, if the day be good; that they can get surer sport, and are less troubled with small fish, by making them rise; and certain it is, that a day when the fish are rising all over the stream is generally one of disappointment.

Another advantage of bank fishing is, that the fish sees the fly only for a moment. He has no long gaze at it, as it comes to him across the water. It either drops exactly over his nose, or sweeps down the stream straight upon him. He expects it to escape on shore the next moment, and chops at it fiercely and hastily, instead of following and examining. Add to this the fact that when he is under the bank there is far less chance of his seeing you; and duly considering these things, you will throw away no more time in drawing, at least in chalk-streams, flies over the watery wastes, to be snapped at now and then by herring-sized pinkeens. In rocky streams, where the quantity of bank food is far smaller, this rule will perhaps not hold good; though who knows not that his best fish are generally taken under some tree from which the little caterpillars, having determined on slow and deliberate suicide, are letting themselves down gently by a silken thread into the mouth of the spotted monarch, who has but to sail about and about, and pick them up one by one as they touch the stream ?—A sight which makes one think—as does a herd of swine crunching acorns, each one of which might have become a 'builder oak'—how Nature is never more magnificent than in her waste.

The next mistake, natural enough to the laziness of fallen man, is that of fishing down-stream, and not up. What Mr. Stewart says on this point should be read by every tyro. By fishing up-stream, even against the wind, he will on an average kill twice as many trout as when fishing down. If trout are out and feeding on the shallows, up or down will simply make the difference of fish or no fish ; and even in deeps, where the difference in the chance of not being seen is not so great, many more fish will be hooked by the man who fishes up-stream, simply because when he strikes he pulls the hook into the trout's mouth instead of out of it. But he who would obey Mr. Stewart in fishing up-stream must obey him also in discarding his light London rod, which is in three cases out of four as weak and 'floppy' in the middle as a waggon whip, and get to himself a stiff and powerful rod, strong enough to spin a minnow; whereby he will obtain, after some weeks of aching muscles, two good things — a fore-arm fit for a sculptor's model, and trout hooked and killed, instead of pricked and lost.

Killed, as well as hooked; for how large trout are to be killed in a weedy chalk-stream without a stiff rod which will take them down, is a question yet unsolved. Even the merest Cockney will know, if he thinks, that weeds float with their points down-stream; and that therefore if a fish is to be brought through them without entangling, he must be 'combed' through them in the same direction. But how is this to be done, if a fish be hooked below you on a weak rod? With a strong rod indeed you can, at the chance of tearing out the hook, keep him by main force on the top of the water, till you have run past him and below him, shortening your line anyhow in loops—there is no time to wind it up with the reel—and then do what you might have done comfortably at first had you been fishing up—viz., bring him down-stream, and let the water run through his gills, and drown him. But with a weak rod—Alas for the tyro! He catches one glimpse of a silver side plunging into the depths; he finds his rod double in his hand; he finds fish and flies stop suddenly somewhere; he rushes down to the spot, sees weeds waving around his line, and guesses from what he feels and sees that the fish is grubbing up-stream through them, five feet under water. He tugs downwards and backwards, but too late; the drop-fly is fast wrapt in Ceratophyllum and Glyceria, Callitriche and Potamogeton, and half-a-dozen more horrid things with long names and longer stems; and what remains but the fate of Campbell's Lord Ullin ?—

> ‘ The waters wild went o'er his child,
> And he was left lamenting.’

Unless, in fact, large fish can be got rapidly down-stream, the chance of killing them is very small; and therefore the man who fishes a willow-fringed brook downward, is worthy of no crown but Ophelia's, besides being likely enough, if he attempt to get down to his fish, to share her fate. The best fisherman, however, will come to shame in streams bordered by pollard willows, and among queer nooks, which can be only fished down-stream. I saw, but the other day, a fish hooked cleverly enough, by throwing to an inch where he ought to have been, and indeed was, and from the only point whence the throw could be made. Out of the water he came, head and tail, the moment he felt the hook, and showed a fair side over two pounds weight . . . . and then ? Instead of running away, he ran right at the fisherman, for reasons which were but too patent. Between man and fish were ten yards of shallow, then a deep weedy shelf, and then the hole which was his house. And for that weedy shelf the spotted monarch made, knowing that there he could drag himself clear of the fly, as perhaps he had done more than once before.

K   G

What was to be done? Take him down-stream through the weed? Alas, on the man's left hand an old pollard leant into the water, barring all downward movement. Jump in and run round? He had rather to run back from the bank, from fear of a loose line; the fish was coming at him so fast that there was no time to wind up. Safe into the weeds hurls the fish; the man, as soon as he finds the fish stop, jumps in mid-leg deep, and staggers up to him, in hopes of clearing; finds the dropper fast in the weeds, and the stretcher, which had been in the fish's mouth, wantoning somewhere in the depths—*Quid plura?* Let us draw a veil over that man's return to shore.

No mortal skill could have killed that fish. Mortal luck (which is sometimes, as most statesmen know, very great) might have done it, if the fish had been irretrievably fast hooked; as, per contra, I once saw a fish of nearly four pounds hooked just above an alder bush, on the same bank as the angler. The stream was swift: there was a great weed-bed above; the man had but about ten feet square of swift water to kill the trout in. Not a foot down-stream could he take him; in fact, he had to pull him hard up-stream to keep him out of his hover in the alder roots. Three times that fish leapt into the air nearly a yard high; and yet, so merciful is luck, and so firmly was he hooked, in five breathless minutes he was in the landing-net;

and when he was there and safe ashore, just of the shape and colour of a silver spoon, his captor lay down panting upon the bank, and with Sir Hugh Evans, manifested 'a great disposition to cry.' But it was a beautiful sight. A sharper round between man and fish never saw I fought in Merry England.

I saw once, however, a cleverer, though not a more dashing feat. A handy little fellow (I wonder where he is now?) hooked a trout of nearly three pounds with his dropper, and at the same moment a post with his stretcher. What was to be done? To keep the fish pulling on him, and not on the post. And that, being favoured by standing on a four-foot bank, he did so well that he tired out the fish in some six feet square of water, stopping him and turning him beautifully whenever he tried to run, till I could get in to him with the landing-net. That was five-and-thirty years since. If the little man has progressed in his fishing as he ought, he should be now one of the finest anglers in England.

*   *   *   *   *

So. Thanks to bank fishing, we have, you see, landed three or four more good fish in the last two hours—And! What is here? An ugly two-pound chub, Chevin, 'Echevin,' or Alderman, as the French call him. How is this, keeper? I thought you allowed no such vermin in this water?

The keeper answers, with a grunt, that ' they allow themselves. That there always were chub hereabouts, and always will be ; for the more he takes out with the net, the more come next day.'

Probably. No nets will exterminate these spawn-eating, fry-eating, all-eating pests, who devour the little trout, and starve the large ones, and, at the first sign of the net, fly to hover among the most tangled roots. There they lie, as close as rats in a bank, and work themselves the farther in the more they are splashed and poked by the poles of the beaters. But the fly, well used, will—if not exterminate them—still thin them down greatly ; and very good sport they give, in my opinion, in spite of the contempt in which they are commonly held, as chicken-hearted fish, who show no fight. True ; but their very cowardice makes them the more difficult to catch ; for no fish must you keep more out of sight, and further off. The very shadow of the line (not to mention that of the rod) sends them flying to hover; and they rise so cautiously and quietly, that they give excellent lessons in patience and nerve to a beginner. If the fly is dragged along the surface, or jerked suddenly from them, they flee from it in terror ; and when they do, after due delibera-tion, take it in, their rise is so quiet, that you can seldom tell whether your fish weighs half a pound or four pounds and a half—unless you, like most beginners, attempt to show your quickness by that most useless exertion, a violent strike. Then, the snapping of your footlink, or—just as likely—of the top of your rod, makes you fully aware, if not of the pluck, at least of the brute strength, of the burly alderman of the waters. No fish, therefore, will better teach the beginner the good old lesson, 'not to frighten a fish before you have tired him.'

For flies—chub will rise greedily at any large palmers, the larger and rougher the better. A red and a grizzled hackle will always take them ; but the best fly of all is an imitation of the black beetle—the 'undertaker' of the London shops. He, too, can hardly be too large, and should be made of a fat body of black wool, with the metallic black feather of a cock's tail wrapped loosely over it. A still better wing is one of the neck feathers of any metallic-plumed bird, e.g., *Phlogophorus Impeyanus*, the Menaul Pheasant, laid flat and whole on the back, to imitate the wing-shells of the beetle, the legs being represented by any loose black feathers—(not hackles, which are too fine.) Tied thus, it will kill not only every chub in a pool (if you give the survivors a quarter of an hour wherein to recover from their horror at their last friend's fate), but also, here and there, very large trout.

Another slur upon the noble sport of chub fishing is the fact of his not being worth eating—a fact which,

in the true sportsman's eyes, will go for nothing. But
though the man who can buy fresh soles and salmon
may despise chub, there are those who do not. True,
you may make a most accurate imitation of him by
taking one of Palmer's patent candles, wick and all,
stuffing it with needles and split bristles, and then
stewing the same in ditch-water. Nevertheless, strange
to say, the agricultural stomach digests chub; and if,
after having filled your creel, or three creels (as you
may too often), with them, you will distribute them
on your way home to all the old women you meet, you
will make many poor souls happy, after having saved
the lives of many trout.

But here we come to a strip of thick cover, part of
our Squire's home preserves, which it is impossible to
fish, so closely do the boughs cover the water. We will
walk on through it towards the hall, and there get—
what we begin sorely to need—something to eat. It
will be of little use fishing for some time to come; for
these hot hours of the afternoon, from three till six,
are generally the ' deadest time ' of the whole day.

And now, when we have struggled in imagination
through the last bit of copse, and tumbled over the
palings into the lawn, we shall see a scene quite as
lovely, if you will believe it, as any alp on earth.

What shall we see, as we look across the broad, still,
clear river, where the great dark trout sail to and fro

lazily in the sun? For having free-warren of our fancy
and our paper, we may see what we choose.

White chalk-fields above, quivering hazy in the heat.
A park full of merry haymakers; gay red and blue
waggons; stalwart horses switching off the flies; dark
avenues of tall elms; groups of abele, 'tossing their
whispering silver to the sun;' and amid them the
house. What manner of house shall it be? Tudor or
Elizabethan, with oriels, mullioned windows, gables,
and turrets of strange shape? No: that is common-
place. Everybody builds Tudor houses now. Our
house shall smack of Inigo Jones or Christopher Wren;
a great square red-brick mass, made light and cheerful
though, by quoins and windows of white Sarsden stone;
with high-peaked French roofs, broken by louvres and
dormers, haunted by a thousand swallows and starlings.
Old walled gardens, gay with flowers, shall stretch right
and left. Clipt yew alleys shall wander away into
mysterious glooms: and out of their black arches shall
come tripping children, like white fairies, to laugh and
talk with the girl who lies dreaming and reading in
the hammock there, beneath the black velvet canopy
of the great cedar-tree, like some fair Tropic flower
hanging from its boughs. Then they shall wander
down across the smooth-shorn lawn, where the purple
rhododendrons hang double, bush and image, over the
water's edge, and call to us across the stream, 'What

sport ?' and the old Squire shall beckon the keeper over the long stone bridge, and return with him bringing luncheon and good ale ; and we will sit down, and eat and drink among the burdock leaves, and then watch the quiet house, and lawn, and flowers, and fair human creatures, and shining water, all sleeping breathless in the glorious light beneath the glorious blue, till we doze off, lulled by the murmur of a thousand insects, and the rich minstrelsy of nightingale and blackcap, thrush and dove.

Peaceful, graceful, complete English country life and country houses ; everywhere finish and polish ; Nature perfected by the wealth and art of peaceful centuries ! Why should I exchange you, even for the sight of all the Alps, for bad roads, bad carriages, bad inns, bad food, bad washing, bad beds, and fleas, fleas, fleas ?

Let that last thought be enough. There may be follies, there may be sorrows, there may be sins—though I know there are no very heavy ones—in that fine old house opposite : but thanks to the genius of my native land, there are at least no fleas.

Think of that, wandering friend ; and of this also, that you will find your warm bath ready when you go to bed to-night, and your cold one when you rise to-morrow morning ; and in content and thankfulness, stay in England, and be clean.

*   *   *   *   *

Here, then, let us lounge a full two hours, too comfortable and too tired to care for fishing, till the hall-bell rings for that dinner which we as good anglers will despise. Then we will make our way to the broad reaches above the house. The evening breeze should be ruffling them gallantly; and see, the fly is getting up. Countless thousands are rising off the grass, and flickering to and fro above the stream. Stand still a moment, and you will hear the air full of the soft rustle of innumerable wings. Hundreds more, even more delicate and gauzy, are rising through the water, and floating helplessly along the surface, as Aphrodite may have done when she rose in the Ægean, half frightened at the sight of the new upper world. And, see, the great trout are moving everywhere. Fish too large and well fed to care for the fly at any other season, who have been lounging among the weeds all day and snapping at passing minnows, have come to the surface; and are feeding steadily, splashing five or six times in succession, and then going down awhile to bolt their mouthful of victims; while here and there a heavy silent swirl tells of a fly taken before it has reached the surface, untimely slain before it has seen the day.

Now—put your Green-drake on; and throw, regardless of bank-fishing or any other rule, wherever you see a fish rise. Do not work your flies in the least, but let them float down over the fish, or sink if they will; he

is more likely to take them under water than on the
top. And mind this rule : be patient with your fish ;
and do not fancy that because he does not rise to you
the first or the tenth time, therefore he will not rise at
all. He may have filled his mouth and gone down to
gorge ; and when he comes up again, if your fly be the
first which he meets, he will probably seize it greedily,
and all the more so if it be under water, so seeming
drowned and helpless. Besides, a fish seldom rises twice
exactly in the same place, unless he be lying between
two weeds, or in the corner of an eddy. His small
wits, when he is feeding in the open, seem to hint to
him that after having found a fly in one place he must
move a foot or two on to find another ; and therefore it
may be some time before your turn comes, and your fly
passes just over his nose ; which if it do not do, he
certainly will not, amid such an abundance, go out of
his way for it. In the meanwhile your footlink will
very probably have hit him over the back, or run foul
of his nose, in which case you will not catch him at all.
A painful fact for you ; but if you could catch every
fish you saw, where would be the trout for next season ?

Put on a dropper of some kind, say a caperer, as a
second chance. I almost prefer the dark claret-spin-
ner, with which I have killed very large fish alternately
with the green-drake, even when it was quite dark ;
and for your stretcher, of course a green-drake.

For a blustering evening like this your drake can hardly be too large or too rough; in brighter and stiller weather the fish often prefer a fly half the size of the natural one. Only bear in mind that the most tempting form among these millions of drakes is that one whose wings are very little coloured at all, of a pale greenish yellow; whose body is straw-coloured, and his head, thorax, and legs, spotted with dark brown—best represented by a pheasant or coch-a-bonddhu hackle.

The best imitation of this, or of any drake, which I have ever seen, is one by Mr. Macgowan, whilome of Ballyshannon, now of No. 7, Bruton-street, Berkeley-square, whose drakes, known by a waxy body of some mysterious material, do surpass those of all other men, and should be known and honoured far and wide. But failing them, you may do well with a drake which is ribbed through the whole length with red hackle over a straw-coloured body. A North-countryman would laugh at it, and ask us how we fancy that fish will mistake for that delicate waxy fly a heavy rough palmer, made heavier and rougher by two thick tufts of yellow mallard wing: but if he will fish therewith, he will catch trout; and mighty ones they will be. I have found, again and again, this drake, in which the hackle is ribbed all down the body, beat a bare-bodied one in the ratio of three fish to one. The reason is difficult to guess. Perhaps the shining transparent hackle gives the fly more of the waxy look of the natural insect; or perhaps the 'buzzly' look of the fly causes the fish to mistake it for one half emerged from its pupa case, fluttering, entangled, and helpless. But whatever be the cause, I am sure of the fact. Now—silence and sport for the next three hours.

     *   *   *   *   *

There! All things must end. It is so dark that I have been fishing for the last five minutes without any end fly; and we have lost our two last fish simply by not being able to guide them into the net. But what an evening's sport we have had! Beside several over a pound which I have thrown in (I trust you have been generous and done likewise), there are six fish averaging two pounds apiece; and what is the weight of that monster with whom I saw you wrestling dimly through the dusk, your legs stuck knee-deep in a mudbank, your head embowered in nettles, while the keeper waltzed round you, roaring mere incoherencies? —four pounds full. Now, is there any sherry left in the flask? No. Then we will give the keeper five shillings; he is well worth his pay; and then drag our weary limbs towards the hall to bath, supper, and bed; while you confess, I trust, that you may get noble sport, hard exercise, and lovely scenery, without going sixty miles from London town.

III.

THE FENS.

III.

THE FENS.

A CERTAIN sadness is pardonable to one who watches the destruction of a grand natural phenomenon, even though its destruction bring blessings to the human race. Reason and conscience tell us, that it is right and good that the Great Fen should have become, instead of a waste and howling wilderness, a garden of the Lord, where

> 'All the land in flowery squares,
> Beneath a broad and equal-blowing wind,
> Smells of the coming summer.'

And yet the fancy may linger, without blame, over the shining meres, the golden reed-beds, the countless water-fowl, the strange and gaudy insects, the wild nature, the mystery, the majesty—for mystery and majesty there were—which haunted the deep fens for many a hundred years. Little thinks the Scotsman, whirled down by the Great Northern Railway from

Peterborough to Huntingdon, what a grand place, even twenty years ago, was that Holme and Whittlesea, which is now but a black, unsightly, steaming flat, from which the meres and reed-beds of the old world are gone, while the corn and roots of the new world have not as yet taken their place.

But grand enough it was, that black ugly place, when backed by Caistor Hanglands and Holme Wood, and the patches of the primæval forest; while dark-green alders, and pale-green reeds, stretched for miles round the broad lagoon, where the coot clanked, and the bittern boomed, and the sedge-bird, not content with its own sweet song, mocked the notes of all the birds around; while high overhead hung, motionless, hawk beyond hawk, buzzard beyond buzzard, kite beyond kite, as far as eye could see. Far off, upon the silver mere, would rise a puff of smoke from a punt, invisible from its flatness and its white paint. Then down the wind came the boom of the great stanchion-gun; and after that sound another sound, louder as it neared; a cry as of all the bells of Cambridge, and all the hounds of Cottesmore; and overhead rushed and whirled the skein of terrified wild-fowl, screaming, piping, clacking, croaking, filling the air with the hoarse rattle of their wings, while clear above all sounded the wild whistle of the curlew, and the trumpet note of the great wild swan.

They are all gone now. No longer do the ruffs trample the sedge into a hard floor in their fighting-rings, while the sober reeves stand round, admiring the tournament of their lovers, gay with ears and tippets, no two of them alike. Gone are ruffs and reeves, spoonbills, bitterns, avosets; the very snipe, one hears, disdains to breed. Gone, too, not only from Whittlesea but from the whole world, is that most exquisite of English butterflies, *Lycœna dispar*—the great copper; and many a curious insect more. Ah, well, at least we shall have wheat and mutton instead, and no more typhus and ague; and, it is to be hoped, no more brandy-drinking and opium-eating; and children will live and not die. For it was a hard place to live in, the old Fen; a place wherein one heard of 'unexampled instances of longevity,' for the same reason that one hears of them in savage tribes—that few lived to old age at all, save those iron constitutions which nothing could break down.

And now, when the bold Fen-men, who had been fighting water by the help of wind, have given up the more capricious element for that more manageable servant fire; have replaced their wind-mills by steam-engines, which will work in all weathers; and have pumped the whole fen dry—even too dry, as the last hot summer proved; when the only bit of the primæval wilderness left, as far as I know, is 200 acres of

K H

sweet sedge and *Lastræa thelypteris* in Wicken Fen: there can be no harm in lingering awhile over the past, and telling of what the Great Fen was, and how it came to be that great flat which reaches (roughly speaking) from Cambridge to Peterborough on the south-west side, to Lynn and Tattershall on the north-east, some forty miles and more each way.

To do that rightly, and describe how the Fen came to be, one must go back, it seems to me, to an age before all history; an age which cannot be measured by years or centuries; an age shrouded in mystery, and to be spoken of only in guesses. To assert anything positively concerning that age, or ages, would be to show the rashness of ignorance. 'I think that I believe,' 'I have good reason to suspect,' 'I seem to see,' are the strongest forms of speech which ought to be used over a matter so vast and as yet so little elaborated.

'I seem to see,' then, an epoch after those strata were laid down with which geology generally deals; after the Kimmeridge clay, Oxford clay, and Gault clay, which form the impervious bedding of the fens, with their intermediate beds of coral-rag and green sand, had been deposited; after the chalk had been laid on the top of them, at the bottom of some ancient ocean; after (and what a gulf of time is implied in that last 'after!') the boulder-clay (coeval

probably with the 'till' of Scotland) had been spread
out in the 'age of ice' on top of all; after the whole
had been upheaved out of the sea, and stood about
the same level as it stands now: but before the great
valley of the Cam had been scooped out, and the
strata were still continuous, some 200 feet above
Cambridge and its colleges, from the top of the Gog-
magogs to the top of Madingley Rise.

In those ages—while the valleys of the Cam, the
Ouse, the Nene, the Welland, the Glen, and the
Witham were sawing themselves out by no violent
convulsions, but simply, as I believe, by the same
slow action of rain and rivers by which they are
sawing backward into the land even now—I 'seem
to see' a time when the Straits of Dover did not
exist—a time when a great part of the German Ocean
was dry land. Through it, into a great estuary between
North Britain and Norway, flowed together all the
rivers of north-eastern Europe—Elbe, Weser, Rhine,
Scheldt, Seine, Thames, and all the rivers of east
England, as far north as the Humber.

And if a reason be required for so daring a theory
—first started, if I recollect right, by the late lamented
Edward Forbes—a sufficient one may be found in one
look over a bridge, in any river of the East of Eng-
land. There we see various species of Cyprinidæ,
'rough' or 'white' fish—roach, dace, chub, bream,

and so forth, and with them their natural attendant and devourer, the pike.

Now these fish belong almost exclusively to the same system of rivers—those of north-east Europe. They attain their highest development in the great lakes of Sweden. Westward of the Straits of Dover they are not indigenous. They may be found in the streams of south and western England; but in every case, I believe, they have been introduced either by birds or by men. From some now submerged 'centre of creation' (to use poor Edward Forbes's formula) they must have spread into the rivers where they are now found; and spread by fresh water, and not by salt, which would destroy them in a single tide.

Again, there lingers in the Cam, and a few other rivers of north-eastern Europe, that curious fish the eel-pout or 'burbot' (*Molva lota*). Now he is utterly distinct from any other fresh-water fish of Europe. His nearest ally is the ling (*Molva vulgaris*); a deep-sea fish, even as his ancestors have been. Originally a deep-sea form, he has found his way up the rivers, even to Cambridge, and there remains. The rivers by which he came up, the land through which he passed, ages and ages since, have been all swept away; and he has never found his way back to his native salt-water, but lives on in a strange land, degraded in form, dwindling in numbers, and now fast dying out. The explanation may be strange: but it is the only one which I can offer to explain the fact—which is itself much more strange—of the burbot being found in the Fen rivers.

Another proof may be found in the presence of the edible frog of the Continent at Foulmire, on the edge of the Cambridge Fens. It is a moot point still with some, whether he was not put there by man. It is a still stronger argument against his being indigenous, that he is never mentioned as an article of food by the mediæval monks, who would have known —Frenchmen, Italians, Germans, as many of them were—that he is as dainty as ever was a spring chicken. But if he be indigenous, his presence proves that once he could either hop across the Straits of Dover, or swim across the German Ocean.

But there can be no doubt of the next proof—the presence in the Fens (where he is now probably extinct) and in certain spots in East Anglia, which I shall take care not to mention, of that exquisite little bird the 'Bearded Tit' (*Calamophilus biarmicus*). Tit he is none; rather, it is said, a finch, but connected with no other English bird. His central home is in the marshes of Russia and Prussia; his food the mollusks which swarm among the reed-beds where he builds; and feeding on those from reed-bed to reed-bed, all across what was once the German Ocean, has come the beautiful little bird with long tail, orange tawny plumage, and black moustache, which might have been seen forty years ago in hundreds on every reed-rond of the Fen.

One more proof—for it is the heaping up of facts, each minute by itself, which issues often in a sound and great result. In draining Wretham Mere, in Norfolk, not so very far from the Fens, in the year 1856 there were found embedded in the peat moss (which is not the Scotch and Western *Sphagnum palustre*, but an altogether different moss, *Hypnum fluitans*), remains of an ancient lake-dwelling, supported on piles. A dwelling like those which have lately attracted so much notice in the lakes of Switzerland: like those which the Dyaks make about the ports and rivers of Borneo ; dwellings invented, it seems to me, to enable the inhabitants to escape not wild beasts only, but malaria and night frosts ; and, perched above the cold and poisonous fogs, to sleep, if not high and dry, at least high and healthy.

In the bottom of this mere were found two shells of the fresh-water tortoise, *Emys lutaria*, till then unknown in England.

These little animals, who may be seen in hundreds in the meres of eastern Europe, sunning their backs on fallen logs, and diving into the water at the sound of a footstep, are eaten largely in continental capitals (as is their cousin the terrapin, *Emys picta*, in the Southern States). They may be bought at Paris, at fashionable restaurants. Thither they may have been sent from Vienna or Berlin; for in north France, Holland, and north-west Germany they are unknown. A few specimens have been found buried in peat in Sweden and Denmark; and there is a tale of a live one having been found in the extreme south part of Sweden, some twenty years ago.[1] Into Sweden, then, as into England, the little fresh-water tortoise had wandered, as to an extreme limit, beyond which the change of climate, and probably of food, killed him off.

But the emys which came to the Wretham bog must have had a long journey; and a journey by fresh water too. Down Elbe or Weser he must have floated, ice-packed, or swept away by flood, till somewhere off the Doggerbank, in that great network of rivers which is now open sea, he or his descendants turned up Ouse and Little Ouse, till they found a mere like their old Prussian one, and there founded a tiny colony for a few generations, till they were eaten up by the savages of the table dwelling; or died out—as many a human family has died out—because they found the world too hard.

---

[1] For these details I am indebted to a paper in the 'Annals of Natural History,' for September 1862, by my friend, Professor Alfred Newton, of Cambridge.

And lastly, my friend Mr. Brady, well known to naturalists, has found that many forms of Entomastraca are common to the estuaries of the east of England and to those of Holland.

It was thus necessary, in order to account for the presence of some of the common animals of the fen, to go back to an epoch of immense remoteness.

And how was that great lowland swept away? Who can tell? Probably by no violent convulsion. Slow upheavals, slow depressions, there may have been— indeed must have been—as the sunken fir-forests of Brancaster, and the raised beach of Hunstanton, on the extreme north-east corner of the Wash, testify to this day. But the main agent of destruction has been, doubtless, that same ever-gnawing sea-wash which devours still the soft strata of the whole east coast of England, as far as Flamborough Head; and that great scavenger, the tide-wave, which sweeps the fallen rubbish out to sea twice in every twenty-four hours. Wave and tide by sea, rain and river by land; these are God's mighty mills in which He makes the old world new. And as Longfellow says of moral things, so may we of physical:—

Though the mills of God grind slowly, yet they grind exceeding
    small.
Though He sit, and wait with patience, with exactness grinds
    He all.'

The lighter and more soluble particles, during that slow but vast destruction which is going on still to this day, have been carried far out to sea, and deposited as ooze. The heavier and coarser have been left along the shores, as the gravels which fill the old estuaries of the east of England.

From these gravels we can judge of the larger animals which dwelt in that old world. About these lost lowlands wandered herds of the woolly mammoth, *Elephas primigenius*, whose bones are common in certain Cambridge gravels, whose teeth are brought up by dredgers, far out in the German Ocean, off certain parts of the Norfolk coast. With them wandered the woolly rhinoceros (*R. tichorhinus*), the hippopotamus, the lion —not (according to some) to be distinguished from the recent lion of Africa—the hyæna, the bear, the horse, the reindeer, and the musk ox ; the great Irish elk, whose vast horns are so well known in every museum of northern Europe ; and that mighty ox, the *Bos primigenius*, which still lingered on the Continent in Cæsar's time, as the urus, in magnitude less only than the elephant,—and not to be confounded with the bison, a relation of, if not identical with, the buffalo of North America,—which still lingers, carefully preserved by the Czar, in the forests of Lithuania.

The remains of this gigantic ox, be it remembered, are found throughout Britain, and even into the Shetland

Isles. Would that any gentleman who may see these pages would take notice of the fact, that we have not (so I am informed) in these islands a single perfect skeleton of *Bos primigenius;* while the Museum of Copenhagen, to its honour, possesses five or six from a much smaller field than is open to us; and be public-spirited enough, the next time he hears of ox-bones, whether in gravel or in peat (as he may in the draining of any northern moss), to preserve them for the museum of his neighbourhood—or send them to Cambridge.

But did all these animals exist at the same time? It is difficult to say. The study of the different gravels is most intricate—almost a special science in itself—in which but two or three men are adepts. It is hard, at first sight, to believe that the hippopotamus could have been the neighbour of the Arctic reindeer and musk ox : but that the woolly mammoth not only may have been such, but was such, there can be no doubt. His remains, imbedded in ice at the mouth of the great Siberian rivers, with the wool, skin, and flesh (in some cases) still remaining on the bones, prove him to have been fitted for a cold climate, and to have browsed upon the scanty shrubs of Northern Asia. But, indeed, there is no reason, *à priori*, why these huge mammals, now confined to hotter countries, should not have once inhabited a colder region, or at least have wandered northwards in

whole herds in summer, to escape insects, and find fresh
food, and above all, water. The same is the case with
the lion, and other huge beasts of prey. The tiger of
Hindostan ranges, at least in summer, across the snows
of the Himalaya, and throughout China. Even at the
river Amoor, where the winters are as severe as at St.
Petersburg, the tiger is an ordinary resident at all
seasons. The lion was, undoubtedly, an inhabitant of
Thrace as late as the expedition of Xerxes, whose
camels they attacked ; and the 'Nemæan lion,' and the
other lions which stand out in Grecian myth, as having
been killed by Hercules and the heroes, may have been
the last remaining specimens of that *Felis spelæa* (un-
distinguishable, according to some, from the African
lion), whose bones are found in the gravels and the
caverns of these isles.

And how long ago were those days of mammoths
and reindeer, lions and hyænas ? We must talk not of
days, but of ages ; we know nothing of days or years.
As the late lamented Professor Sedgwick has well
said :—

'We allow that the great European oscillation, which
ended in the production of the drift (the boulder clay,
or till), was effected during a time of vast, but unknown
length. And if we limit our inquiries, and ask what
was the interval of time between the newest bed of
gravel near Cambridge, and the oldest bed of bog-land

or silt in Cambridgeshire and Norfolk, we are utterly at a loss for a definite answer. The interval of time may have been very great. But we have no scale on which to measure it.'

Let us suppose, then, the era of 'gravels' past; the valleys which open into the fen sawn out by rivers to about their present depth. What was the special cause of the fen itself? why did not the great lowland become a fertile 'carse' of firm alluvial soil, like that of Stirling?

One reason is, that the carse of Stirling has been upheaved some twenty feet, and thereby more or less drained, since the time of the Romans. A fact patent and provable from Cramond (the old Roman port of Alaterna) up to Blair Drummond above Stirling, where whales' skeletons, and bone tools by them, have been found in loam and peat, twenty feet above high-water mark. The alluvium of the fens, on the other hand, has very probably suffered a slight depression.

But the main reason is, that the silt brought down by the fen rivers cannot, like that of the Forth and its neighbouring streams, get safe away to sea. From Flamborough Head, in Yorkshire, all down the Lincolnshire coast, the land is falling, falling for ever into the waves; and swept southward by tide and current, the debris turns into the Wash between Lincolnshire and Norfolk, there to repose, as in a quiet haven.

Hence that vast labyrinth of banks between Lynn and Wisbeach, of mud inside, brought down by the fen rivers; but outside (contrary to the usual rule) of shifting sand, which has come inward from the sea, and prevents the mud's escape—banks parted by narrow gullies, the delight of the gunner with his punt, haunted by million wild-fowl in winter, and in summer hazy steaming flats, beyond which the trees of Lincolnshire loom up, raised by refraction far above the horizon, while the masts and sails of distant vessels quiver, fantastically distorted and lengthened, sometimes even inverted, by a refraction like that which plays such tricks with ships and coasts in the Arctic seas. Along the top of the mud banks lounge the long black rows of seals, undistinguishable from their reflection in the still water below; distorted too, and magnified to the size of elephants. Long lines of sea-pies wing their way along at regular tide-hours, from or to the ocean. Now and then a skein of geese paddle hastily out of sight round a mud-cape; or a brown robber gull (generally Richardson's *Skua*) raises a tumult of screams, by making a raid upon a party of honest white gulls, to frighten them into vomiting up their prey for his benefit; or a single cormorant flaps along, close to the water, towards his fishing ground. Even the fish are shy of haunting a bottom which shifts with every storm; and innumerable shrimps are almost the only product of the shallow

barren sea : beside, all is silence and desolation, **as of** a
world waiting to be made.

So strong is the barrier which these sea-borne sands
oppose to the river-borne ooze, that as soon as a sea-
bank is built—as the projectors of the 'Victoria County'
have built them—across any part of the estuary, the
mud caught by it soon 'warps' the space within into
firm and rich dry land. But that same barrier, ere the
fen was drained, backed up for ages not only the silt,
but the very water of the fens ; and spread it inland into
a labyrinth of shifting streams, shallow meres, and vast
peat bogs, on those impervious clays which floor the fen.
Each river contributed to the formation of those bogs
and meres, instead of draining them away ; repeating on
a huge scale the process which may be seen in many a
highland strath, where the ground at the edge of the
stream is firm and high ; the meadows near the hillfoot,
a few hundred yards away, bogland lower than the
bank of the stream. For each flood deposits its silt
upon the immediate bank of the river, raising it year
by year ; till—as in the case of the 'Levée' of the
Mississippi, and probably of every one of the old fen
rivers—the stream runs at last between two natural
dykes, at a level considerably higher than that of the
now swamped and undrainable lands right and left
of it.

If we add to this, a slope in the fen rivers so ex-

traordinarily slight, that the river at Cambridge is only
thirteen and a half feet above the mean sea level, five-
and-thirty miles away, and that if the great sea-sluice
of Denver, the key of all the eastern fen, were washed
away, the tide would back up the Cam to within ten
miles of Cambridge; if we add again the rainfall upon
that vast flat area, utterly unable to escape through
rivers which have enough to do to drain the hills
around; it is easy to understand how peat, the certain
product of standing water, has slowly overwhelmed the
rich alluvium, fattened by the washing of those phos-
phatic greensand beds, which (discovered by the science
of the lamented Professor Henslow) are now yielding
round Cambridge supplies of manure seemingly inex-
haustible. Easy it is to understand how the all-devour-
ing, yet all-preserving peat-moss swallowed up gradually
the stately forests of fir and oak, ash and poplar, hazel
and yew, which once grew on that rank land; how
trees, torn down by flood or storm, floated and lodged
in rafts, damming the waters back still more; how
streams, bewildered in the flats, changed their channels,
mingling silt and sand with the peat-moss; how Nature,
left to herself, ran into wild riot and chaos more and
more; till the whole fen became one 'Dismal Swamp,'
in which the 'Last of the English' (like Dred in Mrs.
Stowe's tale) took refuge from their tyrants, and lived,
like him, a free and joyous life awhile.

For there were islands, and are still, in that wide fen, which have escaped the destroying deluge of peat-moss; outcrops of firm land, which even in the Middle Age preserved the Fauna and Flora of the primæval forest, haunted by the descendants of some at least of those wild beasts which roamed on the older continent of the 'gravel age.' The all-preserving peat, as well as the monkish records of the early Middle Age, enable us to repeople, tolerably well, the primæval fen.

The gigantic ox, *Bos primigenius,* was still there, though there is no record of him in monkish tales. But with him had appeared (not unknown toward the end of the gravel age) another ox, smaller and with shorter horns, *Bos longifrons;* which is held to be the ancestor of our own domestic short-horns, and of the wild cattle still preserved at Chillingham and at Cadzow. The reindeer had disappeared, almost or altogether. The red deer, of a size beside which the largest Scotch stag is puny, and even the great Carpathian stag inferior, abound; so does the roe, so does the goat, which one is accustomed to look on as a mountain animal. In the Woodwardian Museum there is a portion of a skull of an ibex—probably *Capra sibirica*—which was found in the drift gravel at Fulbourne. Wild sheep are unknown. The horse occurs in the peat; but whether wild or tame, who can tell? Horses enough have been mired and drowned since the Romans set foot on this island, to account for the presence of horses' skulls, without the hypothesis of wild herds, such as doubtless existed in the gravel times. The wolf, of course, is common; wild cat, marten, badger, and otter all would expect; but not so the beaver, which nevertheless is abundant in the peat; and damage enough the busy fellows must have done, cutting trees, damming streams, flooding marshes, and like selfish speculators in all ages, sacrificing freely the public interest to their own. Here and there are found the skulls of bears, in one case that of a polar bear, ice-drifted; and one of a walrus, probably washed in dead after a storm.

Beautiful, after their kind, were these fen-isles, in the eyes of the monks who were the first settlers in the wilderness.

The author of the History of Ramsey grows enthusiastic, and, after the manner of old monks, somewhat bombastic also, as he describes the lonely isle which got its name from the solitary ram who had wandered thither, either in some extreme drought or over the winter ice, and never able to return, was found, fat beyond the wont of rams, feeding among the wild deer. He tells of the stately ashes—most of them cut in his time, to furnish mighty beams for the church roof; of the rich pastures painted with all gay flowers in spring; of the 'green crown' of reed and alder which girdled round the isle; of the fair wide mere with

K   I

its ' sandy beach ' along the forest side : ' a delight,' he says, ' to all who look thereon.'

In like humour, William of Malmesbury, writing in the first half of the twelfth century, speaks of Thorney Abbey and isle. ' It represents,' he says, ' a very Paradise, for that in pleasure and delight it resembles heaven itself. These marshes abound in trees, whose length without a knot doth emulate the stars. The plain there is as level as the sea, which with green grass allures the eye, and so smooth that there is nought to hinder him who runs through it. Neither is therein any waste place : for in some parts are apple trees, in other vines, which are either spread on the ground or raised on poles. A mutual strife is there between nature and art ; so that what one produces not, the other supplies. What shall I say of those fair buildings, which 'tis so wonderful to see the ground among those fens upbear ? '

But the most detailed picture of a fen-isle is that in the second part of the Book of Ely ; wherein a single knight of all the French army forces his way into the isle of St. Etheldreda, and, hospitably entertained there by Hereward and his English, is sent back safe to William the Conqueror, to tell him of the strength of Ely isle.

He cannot praise enough—his speech may be mythical ; but as written by Richard of Ely, only

one generation after, it must describe faithfully what
the place was like—the wonders of the isle : its soil
the richest in England, its pleasant pastures, its noble
hunting-grounds, its store of sheep and cattle (though
its vines, he says, as a Frenchman had good right to
say, were not equally to be praised), its wide meres
and bogs, about it like a wall. In it was, to quote
roughly, 'abundance of tame beasts and of wild stag,
roe, and goat, in grove and marsh ; martens, and
ermines, and fitchets, which in hard winter were
caught in snares or gins. But of the kind of fish
and fowl which bred therein, what can I say? In
the pools around are netted eels innumerable, great
water wolves, and pickerel, perch, roach, burbot,
lampreys, which the French called sea-serpents ;
smelts, too ; and the royal fish, the turbot [surely a
mistake for sturgeon], are said often to be taken.
But of the birds which haunt around, if you be not
tired, as of the rest, we will expound. Innumerable
geese, gulls, coots, divers, water-crows, herons, ducks,
of which, when there is most plenty, in winter, or
at moulting time, I have seen hundreds taken at a
time, by nets, springes, or birdlime,' and so forth ;
till, as he assures William, the Frenchman may sit
on Haddenham field blockading Ely for seven years
more, 'ere they will make one ploughman stop
short in his furrow, one hunter cease to set his nets,

or one fowler to deceive the birds with springe and snare.'

And yet there was another side to the picture. Man lived hard in those days, under dark skies, in houses—even the most luxurious of them—which we should think, from draughts and darkness, unfit for felons' cells. Hardly they lived; and easily were they pleased, and thankful to God for the least gleam of sunshine, the least patch of green, after the terrible and long winters of the Middle Age. And ugly enough those winters must have been, what with snow-storm and darkness, flood and ice, ague and rheumatism; while through the long drear winter nights the whistle of the wind and the wild cries of the water-fowl were translated into the howls of witches and demons; and (as in St. Guthlac's case) the delirious fancies of marsh fever made fiends take hideous shapes before the inner eye, and act fantastic horrors round the old fen-man's bed of sedge.

The Romans seem to have done something toward the draining and embanking of this dismal swamp. To them is attributed the car-dyke, or catch-water drain, which runs for many miles from Peterborough northward into Lincolnshire, cutting off the land waters which flow down from the wolds above. To them, too, is to be attributed the old Roman bank, or 'vallum,' along the sea-face of the marshlands, marked to this day by the names of Walsoken, Walton, and Walpoole. But the English invaders were incapable of following out, even of preserving, any public works. Each village was isolated by its own 'march' of forest; each yeoman all but isolated by the 'eaves-drip,' or green lane round his farm. Each 'cared for his own things, and none for those of others;' and gradually, during the early Middle Age, the fen—save those old Roman villages—returned to its primæval jungle, under the neglect of a race which caricatured local self-government into public anarchy, and looked on every stranger as an alien enemy, who might be lawfully slain, if he came through the forest without calling aloud or blowing a horn. Till late years, the English feeling against the stranger lasted harsh and strong. The farmer, strong in his laws of settlement, tried at once to pass him into the next parish. The labourer, not being versed in law, hove half a brick at him, or hooted him through the town. It was in the fens, perhaps, that the necessity of combined effort for fighting the brute powers of nature first awakened public spirit, and associate labour, and the sense of a common interest between men of different countries and races.

But the progress was very slow; and the first

civilizers of the fen were men who had nothing less in their minds than to conquer nature, or call together round them communities of men. Hermits, driven by that passion for isolated independence which is the mark of the Teutonic mind, fled into the wilderness, where they might, if possible, be alone with God and their own souls. Like St. Guthlac of Crowland, after wild fighting for five-and-twenty years, they longed for peace and solitude; and from their longing, carried out with that iron will which marked the mediæval man for good or for evil, sprang a civilization of which they never dreamed.

Those who wish to understand the old fen life, should read Ingulf's 'History of Crowland' (Mr. Bohn has published a good and cheap translation), and initiate themselves into a state of society, a form of thought, so utterly different from our own, that we seem to be reading of the inhabitants of another planet. Most amusing and most human is old Ingulf and his continuator, 'Peter of Blois;' and though their facts are not to be depended on as having actually happened, they are still instructive, as showing what might, or ought to have happened, in the opinion of the men of old.

Even more naïve is the Anglo-Saxon life of St. Guthlac, written possibly as early as the eighth century, and literally translated by Mr. Goodwin, of Cambridge.

There we may read how the young warrior-noble, Guthlac ('The Battle-Play,' the 'Sport of War'), tired of slaying and sinning, bethought him to fulfil the prodigies seen at his birth; how he wandered into the fen, where one Tatwin (who after became a saint likewise) took him in his canoe to a spot so lonely as to be almost unknown, buried in reeds and alders; and among the trees, nought but an old 'law,' as the Scots still call a mound, which men of old had broken into seeking for treasure, and a little pond; and how he built himself a hermit's cell thereon, and saw visions and wrought miracles; and how men came to him, as to a fakir or shaman of the East; notably one Beccel, who acted as his servant; and how as Beccel was shaving the saint one day, there fell on him a great temptation: Why should he not cut St. Guthlac's throat, and install himself in his cell, that he might have the honour and glory of sainthood? But St. Guthlac perceived the inward temptation (which is told with the naïve honesty of those half-savage times), and rebuked the offender into confession, and all went well to the end.

There we may read, too, a detailed account of a Fauna now happily extinct in the fens: of the creatures

who used to hale St. Guthlac out of his hut, drag him
through the bogs, carry him aloft through frost and
fire—'Develen and luther gostes'—such as tormented
likewise St. Botolph (from whom Botulfston=Boston,
has its name), and who were supposed to haunt the
meres and fens, and to have an especial fondness for
old heathen barrows with their fancied treasure hoards;
how they 'filled the house with their coming, and
poured in on every side, from above, and from beneath,
and everywhere. They were in countenance horrible,
and they had great heads, and a long neck, and a lean
visage; they were filthy and squalid in their beards,
and they had rough ears, and crooked nebs, and fierce
eyes, and foul mouths; and their teeth were like horses'
tusks; and their throats were filled with flame, and
they were grating in their voice; they had crooked
shanks, and knees big and great behind, and twisted
toes, and cried hoarsely with their voices; and they
came with such immoderate noise and immense horror,
that him thought all between heaven and earth
resounded with their voices. . . . . And they tugged
and led him out of the cot, and led him to the swart
fen, and threw and sunk him in the muddy waters.
After that they brought him into the wild places of the
wilderness, among the thick beds of brambles, that all
his body was torn. . . . . After that they took him and
beat him with iron whips; and after that they brought

him on their creaking wings between the cold regions
of the air.'

But there are gentler and more human touches in that
old legend.   You may read in it, how all the wild birds
of the fen came to St. Guthlac, and he fed them after
their kind.   How the ravens tormented him, stealing
letters, gloves, and what not, from his visitors; and then,
seized with compunction at his reproofs, brought them
back, or hanged them on the reeds; and how, as Wilfrid,
a holy visitant, was sitting with him, discoursing of
the contemplative life, two swallows came flying in,
and lifted up their song, sitting now on the saint's hand,
now on his shoulder, now on his knee.   And how, when
Wilfrid wondered thereat, Guthlac made answer, 'Know
you not that he who hath led his life according to
God's will, to him the wild beasts and the wild birds
draw the more near.'

After fifteen years of such a life, in fever, agues, and
starvation, no wonder if St. Guthlac died.   They buried
him in a leaden coffin (a grand and expensive luxury
in the seventh century) which had been sent to him
during his life by a Saxon princess; and then, over his
sacred and wonder-working corpse, as over that of a
Buddhist saint, there rose a chapel, with a community
of monks, companies of pilgrims who came to worship,
sick who came to be healed; till, at last, founded on
great piles driven into the bog, arose the lofty wooden

Abbey of Crowland; in its sanctuary of the four rivers,
its dykes, parks, vineyards, orchards, rich ploughlands,
from which, in time of famine, the monks of Crow-
land fed all people of the neighbouring fens; with
its tower with seven bells, which had not their like
in England; its twelve altars rich with the gifts of
Danish Vikings and princes, and even with twelve
white bear-skins, the gift of Canute's self; while
all around were the cottages of the corrodiers, or folk
who, for a corrody, or life pittance from the abbey,
had given away their lands, to the wrong and detriment
of their heirs.

But within these four rivers, at least, was neither
tyranny nor slavery. Those who took refuge in St.
Guthlac's peace from cruel lords must keep his peace
toward each other, and earn their living like honest
men, safe while they did so; for between those four
rivers St. Guthlac and his abbot were the only lords,
and neither summoner, nor sheriff of the king, nor
armed force of knight or earl, could enter 'the inherit-
ance of the Lord, the soil of St. Mary and St. Bartho-
lomew, the most holy sanctuary of St. Guthlac and
his monks; the minster free from worldly servitude;
the special almshouse of most illustrious kings; the
sole refuge of anyone in worldly tribulation; the
perpetual abode of the saints; the possession of
religious men, specially set apart by the common

council of the realm; by reason of the frequent
miracles of the holy confessor St. Guthlac, an ever-
fruitful mother of camphire in the vineyards of
Eugedi; and by reason of the privileges granted
by the kings, a city of grace and safety to all who
repent.'

Does not all this sound—as I said just now—like a
voice from another planet ? It is all gone; and it was
good and right that it should go when it had done
its work, and that the civilization of the fen should
be taken up and carried out by men like the good
knight, Richard of Rulos, who, two generations after
the Conquest, marrying Hereward's granddaughter, and
becoming Lord of Deeping (the deep meadow), thought
that he could do the same work from the hall of Bourne
as the monks did from their cloisters; got permission
from the Crowland monks, for twenty marks of silver,
to drain as much as he could of the common marshes;
and then shut out the Welland by strong dykes, built
cottages, marked out gardens, and tilled fields, till
'out of slough and bogs accursed, he made a garden of
pleasure.'

Yet one lasting work those monks of Crowland did,
besides those firm dykes and rich corn lands of the
Porsand, which endure unto this day. For within two
generations of the Norman conquest, while the old
wooden abbey, destroyed by fire, was being replaced

by that noble pile of stone whose ruins are still standing, the French abbot of Crowland sent French monks to open a school under the new French donjon, in the little Roman town of Grante-brigge ; whereby —so does all earnest work, however mistaken, grow and spread in this world, infinitely and for ever—St. Guthlac, by his canoe-voyage into Crowland Island, became the spiritual father of the University of Cambridge in the old world; and therefore of her noble daughter, the University of Cambridge, in the new world which fen-men, sailing from Boston deeps, colonized and Christianized, 800 years after St. Guthlac's death.

The drainage of the fens struggled on for these same 800 years slowly, and often disastrously. Great mistakes were made ; as when a certain bishop, some 700 years ago, bethought him to make a cut from Littleport drain to Rebeck (or Priests'-houses), and found, to his horror and that of the fen-men, that he had let down upon Lynn the pent-up waters of the whole higher bogs; that rivers were running backwards, brooks swelling to estuaries, and the whole north-eastern fen ruinate, to be yet more ruinate by banks confusedly thrown up in self-defence, till some order was restored in 1332, and the fens prospered —such little of them as could be drained at all— for nigh two hundred years. Honour, meanwhile, to another prelate, good Bishop Morton, who cut the great leam from Guyhirn—the last place at which one could see a standing gallows, and two Irish reapers hanging in chains, having murdered the old witch of Guyhirn for the sake of hidden treasure, which proved to be some thirty shillings and a few silver spoons.

The belief is more general than well-founded that the drainage of the fens retrograded on account of the dissolution of the monasteries. The state of decay into which those institutions had already fallen, and which alone made their dissolution possible, must have extended itself to these fen-lands. No one can read the account of their debts, neglect, malversation of funds, in the time of Henry VIII., without seeing that the expensive works necessary to keep fen-lands dry must have suffered, as did everything else belonging to the convents.

It was not till the middle or end of Elizabeth's reign that the recovery of these 'drowned lands' was proceeded with once more; and during the first half of the seventeenth century there went on, more and more rapidly, that great series of artificial works which, though often faulty in principle, often unexpectedly disastrous in effect, have got the work done, as all work is done in this world, not as well as it should have been done, but at least done.

To comprehend those works would be impossible without maps and plans; to take a lively interest in them impossible, likewise, save to an engineer or a fenman. Suffice it to say, that in the early part of the seventeenth century we find a great company of adventurers—more than one Cromwell among them, and Francis, the great and good Earl of Bedford, at their head—trying to start a great scheme for draining the drowned 'middle level' east of the Isle of Ely. How they sent for Vermuyden, the Dutchman, who had been draining in North Lincolnshire, about Goole and Axholme Isle; how they got into his hands, and were ruined by him; how Francis of Bedford had to sell valuable estates to pay his share; how the fen-men looked on Francis of Bedford as their champion; how Charles I. persecuted him meanly, though indeed Bedford had, in the matter of the 'Lynn Law' of 1630, given way, as desperate men are tempted to do, to something like sharp practice unworthy of him; how Charles took the work into his hands, and made a Government job of it; how Bedford died, and the fen-men looked on him as a martyr; how Oliver Cromwell arose to avenge the good earl, as his family had supported him in past times; how Oliver St. John came to the help of the fen-men, and drew up the so-called 'Pretended Ordinance' of 1649, which was a compromise between Vermuyden and the adventurers, so able and useful that Charles II.'s Government were content to call it 'pretended' and let it stand, because it was actually draining the fens; and how Sir Cornelius Vermuyden, after doing mighty works, and taking mighty moneys, died a beggar, writing petitions which never got answered; how William, Earl of Bedford, added, in 1649, to his father's 'old Bedford River' that noble parallel river, the Hundred foot, both rising high above the land between dykes and 'washes,' *i.e.* waste spaces right and left, to allow for flood water; how the Great Bedford Rivers silted up the mouth of the Ouse, and backed the floods up the Cam ; how Denver sluice was built to keep them back ; and so forth,—all is written, or rather only half or quarter written, in the histories of the fens.

Another matter equally, or even more important, is but half written—indeed, only hinted at—the mixed population of the fens.

The sturdy old 'Girvii,' 'Gyrwas,' men of the 'gyras' or marshes, who in Hereward's time sang their three-man glees, 'More Girviorum tripliciter canentes,' had been crossed with the blood of Scandinavian Vikings in Canute's conquest; crossed again with English refugees from all quarters during the French conquest under William. After the St. Bartholomew they received a fresh cross of Huguenot, fleeing from France—dark-haired, fiery, earnest folk, whose names and physiognomies are said still to remain about Wisbeach, Whittlesea, and Thorney. Then came Vermuyden's Dutchmen, leaving some of their blood behind them. After the battle of Dunbar another cross came among them, of Scotch prisoners, who, employed by Cromwell's Government on the dykes, settled down among the fen-men to this day. Within the memory of man, Scotchmen used to come down into the fens every year, not merely for harvest, but to visit their expatriated kinsmen.

To these successive immigrations of strong Puritan blood, more than even the influence of the Cromwells and other Puritan gentlemen, we may attribute that strong Calvinist element which has endured for now nigh three centuries in the fen ; and attribute, too, that sturdy independence and self-help which drove them of old out of Boston town, to seek their fortunes first in Holland, then in Massachusetts over sea. And that sturdy independence and self-help is not gone. There still lives in them some of the spirit of their mythic giant Hickafrid (the Hickathrift of nursery rhymes), who, when the Marshland men (possibly the Romanized inhabitants of the wall villages) quarrelled with him in the field, took up the cart-axle for a club, smote them hip and thigh, and pastured his cattle in their despite in the green cheese-fens of the Smeeth. No one has ever seen a fen-bank break, without honouring the

stern quiet temper which there is in these men, when
the north-easter is howling above, the spring-tide roar-
ing outside, the brimming tide-way lapping up to the
dyke-top, or flying over in sheets of spray; when round
the one fatal thread which is trickling over the dyke—
or worse, through some forgotten rat's hole in its side—
hundreds of men are clustered, without tumult, without
complaint, marshalled under their employers, fighting
the brute powers of nature, not for their employer's
sake alone, but for the sake of their own year's labour
and their own year's bread. The sheep have been
driven off the land below; the cattle stand ranged
shivering on high dykes inland; they will be saved in
punts, if the worst befall. But a hundred spades,
wielded by practised hands, cannot stop that tiny rat-
hole. The trickle becomes a rush—the rush a roaring
waterfall. The dyke-top trembles—gives. The men
make efforts, desperate, dangerous, as of sailors in a
wreck, with faggots, hurdles, sedge, turf: but the bank
will break; and slowly they draw off; sullen, but un-
complaining; beaten, but not conquered. A new cry
rises among them. Up, to save yonder sluice; that
will save yonder lode; that again yonder farm; that
again some other lode, some other farm, far back in-
land, but guessed at instantly by men who have studied
from their youth, as the necessity of their existence,
the labyrinthine drainage of lands which are all below

K   K

the water level, and where the inner lands, in many cases, are lower still than those outside.

So they hurry away to the nearest farms; the teams are harnessed, the waggons filled, and drawn down and emptied; the beer-cans go round cheerily, and the men work with a sort of savage joy at being able to do something, if not all, and stop the sluice on which so much depends. As for the outer land, it is gone past hope; through the breach pours a roaring salt cataract, digging out a hole on the inside of the bank, which remains as a deep sullen pond for years to come. Hundreds, thousands of pounds are lost already, past all hope. Be it so, then. At the next neap, perhaps, they will be able to mend the dyke, and pump the water out; and begin again, beaten but not conquered, the same everlasting fight with wind and wave which their forefathers have waged for now 800 years.

He who sees—as I have seen—a sight like that, will repine no more that the primæval forest is cut down, the fair mere drained. For instead of mammoth and urus, stag and goat, that fen feeds cattle many times more numerous than all the wild venison of the pri-mæval jungle; and produces crops capable of nourishing a hundred times as many human beings; and more —it produces men a hundred times as numerous as ever it produced before; more healthy and long-lived —and if they will, more virtuous and more happy—

than ever was Girvian in his log-canoe, or holy hermit in his cell. So we, who knew the deep fen, will breathe one sigh over the last scrap of wilderness, and say no more; content to know that—

> 'The old order changeth, yielding place to new,
> And God fulfils himself in many ways,
> Lest one good custom should corrupt the world.'

IV.

MY WINTER-GARDEN.

IV.

MY WINTER GARDEN.[1]

So, my friend: you ask me to tell you how I contrive
to support this monotonous country life ; how, fond
as I am of excitement, adventure, society, scenery, art,
literature, I go cheerfully through the daily routine of a
commonplace country profession, never requiring a six-
weeks' holiday ; not caring to see the Continent, hardly
even to spend a day in London ; having never yet
actually got to Paris.

You wonder why I do not grow dull as those round
me, whose talk is of bullocks—as indeed mine is, often
enough ; why I am not by this time 'all over blue
mould ;' why I have not been tempted to bury
myself in my study, and live a life of dreams among
old books.

I will tell you. I am a minute philosopher : though
one, thank Heaven, of a different stamp from him whom
the great Bishop Berkeley silenced—alas ! only for

---

[1] *Fraser's Magazine*, January 1858.

a while. I am possibly, after all, a man of small
mind, content with small pleasures. So much the
better for me. Meanwhile, I can understand your sur-
prise, though you cannot understand my content. You
have played a greater game than mine; have lived a
life, perhaps more fit for an Englishman; certainly more
in accordance with the taste of our common fathers, the
Vikings, and their patron Odin 'the goer,' father of all
them that go ahead. You have gone ahead, and over
many lands; and I reverence you for it, though I envy
you not. You have commanded a regiment—indeed an
army, and 'drank delight of battle with your peers;'
you have ruled provinces, and done justice and judg-
ment, like a noble Englishman as you are, old friend,
among thousands who never knew before what justice
and judgment were. You have tasted (and you have
deserved to taste) the joy of old David's psalm, when he
has hunted down the last of the robber lords of Pales-
tine. You have seen 'a people whom you have not
known, serve you. As soon as they heard of you, they
obeyed you; but the strange children dissembled with
you:' yet before you, too, 'the strange children failed,
and trembled in their hill-forts.'

Noble work that was to do, and nobly you have done
it; and I do not wonder that to a man who has been
set to such a task, and given power to carry it through,
all smaller work must seem paltry; that such a man's

very amusements, in that grand Indian land, and that
free adventurous Indian life, exciting the imagination,
calling out all the self-help and daring of a man, should
have been on a par with your work; that when you go
a sporting, you ask for no meaner preserve than the
primæval forest, no lower park wall than the snow-
peaks of the Himalaya.

Yes; you have been a 'burra Shikarree' as well as
a 'burra Sahib.' You have played the great game in
your work, and killed the great game in your play.
How many tons of mighty monsters have you done to
death, since we two were schoolboys together, five-and-
twenty years ago? How many starving villages have
you fed with the flesh of elephant or buffalo? How
many have you delivered from man-eating tigers, or
wary old alligators, their craws full of poor girls' ban-
gles? Have you not been charged by rhinoceroses, all
but ript up by boars? Have you not seen face to face
Ovis Ammon himself, the giant mountain sheep—pri-
mæval ancestor, perhaps, of all the flocks on earth?
Your memories must be like those of Theseus and
Hercules, full of slain monsters. Your brains must be
one fossiliferous deposit, in which gaur and sambur, hog
and tiger, rhinoceros and elephant, lie heaped together,
as the old ichthyosaurs and plesiosaurs are heaped in
the lias rocks at Lyme. And therefore I like to
think of you. I try to picture your feelings to myself.

I spell over with my boy Mayne Reid's amusing books, or the 'Old Forest Ranger,' or Williams's old 'Tiger Book,' with Howitt's plates; and try to realize the glory of a burra Shikarree: and as I read and imagine, feel, with Sir Hugh Evans, 'a great disposition to cry.'

For there were times, full many a year ago, when my brains were full of bison and grizzly bear, mustang and big-horn, Blackfoot and Pawnee, and hopes of wild adventure in the Far West, which I shall never see; for ere I was three-and-twenty, I discovered, plainly enough, that my lot was to stay at home and earn my bread in a very quiet way; that England was to be henceforth my prison or my palace, as I should choose to make it: and I have made it, by Heaven's help, the latter.

I will confess to you, though, that in those first heats of youth, this little England — or rather, this little patch of moor in which I have struck roots as firm as the wild fir-trees do—looked at moments rather like a prison than a palace; that my foolish young heart would sigh, 'Oh! that I had wings'—not as a dove, to fly home to its nest and croodle there—but as an eagle, to swoop away over land and sea, in a rampant and self-glorifying fashion, on which I now look back as altogether unwholesome and undesirable. But the thirst for adventure and excitement was strong in me, as perhaps it ought to be in all at twenty-one. Others went out to see the glorious new worlds of the West, the glorious old worlds of the East—why should not I? Others rambled over Alps and Apennines, Italian picture-galleries and palaces, filling their minds with fair memories—why should not I? Others discovered new wonders in botany and zoology—why should not I? Others too, like you, fulfilled to the utmost that strange lust after the burra shikar, which even now makes my pulse throb as often as I see the stags' heads in our friend A——'s hall: why should not I? It is not learnt in a day, the golden lesson of the Old Collect, to 'love the thing which is commanded, and desire that which is promised.' Not in a day: but in fifteen years one can spell out a little of its worth; and when one finds one's self on the wrong side of forty, and the first grey hairs begin to show on the temples, and one can no longer jump as high as one's third button—scarcely, alas! to any button at all; and what with innumerable sprains, bruises, soakings, and chillings, one's lower limbs feel in a cold thaw much like an old post-horse's, why, one makes a virtue of necessity: and if one still lusts after sights, takes the nearest, and looks for wonders, not in the Himalayas or Lake Ngami, but in the turf on the lawn and the brook in the park; and with good Alphonse Karr enjoys the macro-microcosm in one 'Tour autour de mon jardin.'

For there it is, friend, the whole infinite miracle of nature in every tuft of grass, if we have only eyes to see it, and can disabuse our minds of that tyrannous phantom of size. Only recollect that great and small are but relative terms; that in truth nothing is great or small, save in proportion to the quantity of creative thought which has been exercised in making it; that the fly who basks upon one of the trilithons of Stonehenge, is in truth infinitely greater than all Stonehenge together, though he may measure the **tenth** of an inch, and the stone on which he sits five-and-twenty feet. You differ from me? Be it so. Even if you prove me wrong I will believe myself in the right: I cannot afford to do otherwise. If you rob me of my faith in 'minute philosophy,' you rob me of a continual source of content, surprise, delight.

So go your way and I mine, each working with all his might, and playing with all his might, in his own place and way. Remember only, that though I never can come round to your sphere, you must some day come round to me, when wounds, or weariness, or merely, as I hope, a healthy old age, shall shut you out for once and for all from burra shikar, whether human or quadruped.—For you surely will not take to politics in your old age? You will not surely live to solicit (as many a fine fellow, alas! did but last year) the votes, not even of the people, but merely of the snobocracy, on the ground of your having neither policy nor principles, nor even opinions, upon any matter in heaven or earth?—Then in that day will you be forced, my friend, to do what I have done this many a year; to refrain your soul, and keep it low. You will see more and more the depth of human ignorance, the vanity of human endeavours. You will feel more and more that the world is going God's way, and not yours, or mine, or any man's; and that if you have been allowed to do good work on earth, that work is probably as different from what you fancy it as the tree is from the seed whence it springs. You will grow content, therefore, not to see the real fruit of your labours; because if you saw it you would probably be frightened at it, and what is very good in the eyes of God would not be very good in yours; content, also, to receive your discharge, and work and fight no more, sure that God is working and fighting, whether you are in hospital or in the field. And with this growing sense of the pettiness of human struggles will grow on you a respect for simple labours, a thankfulness for simple pleasures, a sympathy with simple people, and possibly, my trusty friend, with me and my little tours about that moorland which I call my winter-garden, and which is to me as full of glory and of in-struction as the Himalaya or the Punjab are to you, and in which I contrive to find as much health and amusement as I have time for—and who ought to have more?

I call the said garden mine, not because I own it in any legal sense (for only in a few acres have I a life interest), but in that higher sense in which ten thousand people can own the same thing, and yet no man's right interfere with another's. To whom does the Apollo Belvedere belong, but to all who have eyes to see its beauty? So does my winter-garden; and therefore to me among the rest.

Besides (which is a gain to a poor man) my pleasure in it is a very cheap one. So are all those of a minute philosopher, except his microscope. But my winter-garden, which is far larger, at all events, than that famous one at Chatsworth, costs me not one penny in keeping up. Poor, did I call myself? Is it not true wealth to have all I want without paying for it? Is it not true wealth, royal wealth, to have some twenty gentlemen and noblemen, nay, even royal personages, planting and improving for me? Is it not more than royal wealth to have sun and frost, Gulf-stream and south-westers, laws of geology, phytology, physiology, and other ologies—in a word, the whole universe and the powers thereof, day and night, paving, planting, roofing, lighting, colouring my winter-garden for me, without my even having the trouble to rub a magic ring and tell the genii to go to work?

Yes. I am very rich, as every man may be who will. In the doings of our little country neighbourhood I find tragedy and comedy, too fantastic, sometimes too sad, to be written down. In the words of those whose talk is of bullocks, I find the materials of all possible metaphysic, and long weekly that I had time to work them out. In fifteen miles of moorland I find the materials of all possible physical science, and long that I had time to work out one smallest segment of that great sphere. How can I be richer, if I have lying at my feet all day a thousand times more wealth than I can use?

Some people—most people—in these run-about railway days, would complain of such a life, in such a ' narrow sphere,' so they call it, as monotonous. Very likely it is so. But is it to be complained of on that account? Is monotony in itself an evil? Which is better, to know many places ill, or to know one place well? Certainly—if a scientific habit of mind be a gain—it is only by exhausting as far as possible the significance of an individual phenomenon (is not that sentence a true scientific one in its magniloquence?) that you can discover any glimpse of the significance of the universal. Even men of boundless knowledge, like Humboldt, must have had once their speciality, their pet subject, or they would have, strictly speaking, no knowledge at all. The volcanoes of Mexico, patiently and laboriously investigated in his youth, were to Humboldt, possibly, the key of the whole Cosmos. I learn more, studying over and over again the same Bagshot sand and gravel heaps, than I should by roaming all Europe in search of new geologic wonders. Fifteen years have I been puzzling at the same questions and have only guessed at a few of the answers. What sawed out the edges of the moors into long narrow banks of gravel? What cut them off all flat atop? What makes *Erica Tetralix* grow in one soil, and the bracken in another? How did three species of Club-moss—one of them quite an Alpine one—get down here, all the way from Wales perhaps, upon this isolated patch of gravel? Why did that one patch of *Carex arenaria* settle in the only square yard for miles and miles which bore sufficient resemblance to its native sandhill by the seashore, to make it comfortable? Why did *Myosurus minimus*, which I had hunted for in vain for fourteen years, appear by dozens in the fifteenth, upon a new-made bank, which had been for at least two hundred years a farm-yard gateway? Why does it generally rain here from the south-west, not when the barometer falls, but when it begins to rise again? Why—why is everything, which lies under my feet all day long? I don't know; and you can't tell me. And till I have found out, I cannot complain of monotony, with still undiscovered puzzles waiting to be explained, and so to create novelty at every turn.

Besides, monotony is pleasant in itself; morally pleasant, and morally useful. Marriage is monotonous: but there is much, I trust, to be said in favour of holy wedlock. Living in the same house is monotonous: but three removes, say the wise, are as bad as a fire. Locomotion is regarded as an evil by our Litany. The Litany, as usual, is right. 'Those who travel by land or sea' are to be objects of our pity and our prayers; and I do pity them. I delight in that same monotony. It saves curiosity, anxiety, excitement, disappointment, and a host of bad passions. It gives a man the blessed, invigorating feeling that he is at home; that he has roots, deep and wide, struck down into all he sees; and that only The Being who will do nothing cruel or useless can tear them up. It is pleasant to look down on the same parish day after day, and say, I know all that lies beneath, and all beneath know me. If I want a friend, I know where to find him; if I want work done, I know who will do it. It is pleasant and good to see the same trees year after year; the same birds coming back in spring to the same shrubs; the same banks covered with the same flowers, and broken (if they be stiff ones) by the same gaps. Pleasant and good it is to ride the same horse, to sit in the same chair, to wear the same old coat. That man who offered twenty pounds' reward

K

L

for a lost carpet-bag full of old boots was a sage, and I wish I knew him. Why should one change one's place, any more than one's wife or one's children? Is a hermit-crab, slipping his tail out of one strange shell into another, in the hopes of its fitting him a little better, either a dignified, safe, or graceful animal? No; George Riddler was a true philosopher.

> 'Let vules go sarching vur and nigh,
> We bides at Whum, my dog and I;'

and become there, not only wiser, but more charitable; for the oftener one sees, the better one knows; and the better one knows, the more one loves.

It is an easy philosophy; especially in the case of the horse, where a man cannot afford more than one, as I cannot. To own a stud of horses, after all, is not to own horses at all, but riding-machines. Your rich man who rides Crimæa in the morning, Sir Guy in the afternoon, and Sultan to-morrow, and something else the next day, may be a very gallant rider: but it is a question whether he enjoys the pleasure which one horse gives to the poor man who rides him day after day; one horse, who is not a slave, but a friend; who has learnt all his tricks of voice, hand, heel, and knows what his master wants, even without being told; who will bear with his master's infirmities, and feels secure that his master will bear with his in turn.

Possibly, after all, the grapes are sour; and were one rich, one would do even as the rich are wont to do : but still, I am a minute philosopher. And therefore, this afternoon, after I have done the same work, visited the same people, and said the same words to them, which I have done for years past, and shall, I trust, for many a year to come, I shall go wandering out into the same winter-garden on the same old mare; and think the same thoughts, and see the same fir-trees, and meet perhaps the same good fellows hunting of their fox, as I have done with full content this many a year; and rejoice, as I said before, in my own boundless wealth, who have the whole universe to look at, without being charged one penny for the show.

As I have said, the grapes may be sour, and I enjoy the want of luxuries only because I cannot get them; but if my self-deception be useful to me, leave it alone.

No one is less inclined to depreciate that magnificent winter-garden at the Crystal Palace : yet let me, if I choose, prefer my own; I argue that, in the first place, it is far larger. You may drive, I hear, through the grand one at Chatsworth for a quarter of a mile. You may ride through mine for fifteen miles on end. I prefer, too, to any glass roof which Sir Joseph Paxton ever planned, that dome above my head some three miles high, of soft dappled grey and yellow cloud, through the vast lattice-work whereof the blue sky peeps, and sheds down tender gleams on yellow bogs, and softly rounded heather knolls, and pale chalk ranges gleaming far away. But, above all, I glory in my evergreens. What winter-garden can compare for them with mine? True, I have but four kinds—Scotch fir, holly, furze, and the heath; and by way of relief to them, only brows of brown fern, sheets of yellow bog-grass, and here and there a leafless birch, whose purple tresses are even more lovely to my eye than those fragrant green ones which she puts on in spring. Well: in painting as in music, what effects are more grand than those produced by the scientific combination, in endless new variety, of a few simple elements? Enough for me is the one purple birch; the bright hollies round its stem sparkling with scarlet beads; the furze-patch, rich with its lacework of interwoven light and shade, tipped here and there with a golden bud; the deep soft heather carpet, which invites you to lie down and dream for hours; and behind all, the wall of red fir-stems, and the dark fir-roof with its jagged edges a mile long, against the soft grey sky.

An ugly, straight-edged, monotonous fir-plantation? Well, I like it, outside and inside. I need no saw-edge of mountain peaks to stir up my imagination with the sense of the sublime, while I can watch the saw-edge of those fir peaks against the red sunset. They are my Alps; little ones it may be: but after all, as I

asked before, what is size? A phantom of our brain;
an optical delusion. Grandeur, if you will consider
wisely, consists in form, and not in size : and to the
eye of the philosopher, the curve drawn on a paper two
inches long, is just as magnificent, just as symbolic of
divine mysteries and melodies, as when embodied in
the span of some cathedral roof. Have you eyes to see?
Then lie down on the grass, and look near enough to
see something more of what is to be seen; and you
will find tropic jungles in every square foot of turf;
mountain cliffs and debacles at the mouth of every
rabbit burrow : dark strids, tremendous cataracts, 'deep
glooms and sudden glories,' in every foot-broad rill
which wanders through the turf. All is there for you
to see, if you will but rid yourself of 'that idol of
space;' and Nature, as everyone will tell you who
has seen dissected an insect under the microscope, is
as grand and graceful in her smallest as in her hugest
forms.

The March breeze is chilly : but I can be always
warm if I like in my winter-garden. I turn my horse's
head to the red wall of fir-stems, and leap over the
furze-grown bank into my cathedral, wherein if there
be no saints, there are likewise no priestcraft and no
idols; but endless vistas of smooth red green-veined
shafts holding up the warm dark roof, lessening away
into endless gloom, paved with rich brown fir-needle—

a carpet at which Nature has been at work for forty years. Red shafts, green roof, and here and there a pane of blue sky—neither Owen Jones nor Willement can improve upon that ecclesiastical ornamentation,—while for incense I have the fresh healthy turpentine fragrance, far sweeter to my nostrils than the stifling narcotic odour which fills a Roman Catholic cathedral. There is not a breath of air within: but the breeze sighs over the roof above in a soft whisper. I shut my eyes and listen. Surely that is the murmur of the summer sea upon the summer sands in Devon far away. I hear the innumerable wavelets spend themselves gently upon the shore, and die away to rise again. And with the innumerable wave-sighs come innumerable memories, and faces which I shall never see again upon this earth. I will not tell even you of that, old friend.

It has two notes, two keys rather, that Eolian-harp of fir-needles above my head; according as the wind is east or west, the needles dry or wet. This easterly key of to-day is shriller, more cheerful, warmer in sound, though the day itself be colder: but grander still, as well as softer, is the sad soughing key in which the south-west wind roars on, rain-laden, over the forest, and calls me forth—being a minute philosopher —to catch trout in the nearest chalk-stream.

The breeze is gone a while; and I am in perfect silence—a silence which may be heard. Not a sound;

and not a moving object; absolutely none. The
absence of animal life is solemn, startling. That ring-
dove, who was cooing half a mile away, has hushed his
moan; that flock of long-tailed titmice, which were
twinging and pecking about the fir-cones a few minutes
since, are gone: and now there is not even a gnat to
quiver in the slant sun-rays. Did a spider run over
these dead leaves, I almost fancy I could hear his foot-
fall. The creaking of the saddle, the soft step of the
mare upon the fir-needles, jar my ears. I seem alone
in a dead world. A dead world: and yet so full of life,
if I had eyes to see! Above my head every fir-needle
is breathing—breathing for ever; currents unnumbered
circulate in every bough, quickened by some undis-
covered miracle; around me every fir-stem is distilling
strange juices, which no laboratory of man can make;
and where my dull eye sees only death, the eye of God
sees boundless life and motion, health and use.

Slowly I wander on beneath the warm roof of the
winter-garden, and meditate upon that one word—Life;
and specially on all that Mr. Lewes has written so well
thereon—for instance—

'We may consider Life itself as an ever-increasing identification
with Nature. The simple cell, from which the plant or animal arises,
must draw light and heat from the sun, nutriment from the surrounding
world, or else it will remain quiescent, not alive, though latent with
life; as the grains in the Egyptian tombs, which after lying thousands
of years in those sepulchres, are placed in the earth, and smile forth

as golden wheat. What we call growth, is it not a perpetual absorption of Nature, the identification of the individual with the universal? And may we not, in speculative moods, consider Death as the grand impatience of the soul to free itself from the circle of individual activity—the yearning of the creature to be united with the Creator?

'As with Life, so with knowledge, which is intellectual life. In the early days of man's history, Nature and her marvellous ongoings were regarded with but a casual and careless eye, or else with the merest wonder. It was late before profound and reverent study of her laws could wean man from impatient speculations; and now, what is our intellectual activity based on, except on the more thorough mental absorption of Nature? When that absorption is completed, the mystic drama will be sunny clear, and all Nature's processes be visible to man, as a Divine Effluence and Life.'

True: yet not all the truth. But who knows all the truth?

Not I. 'We see through a glass darkly,' said St. Paul of old; and what is more, dazzle and weary our eyes, like clumsy microscopists, by looking too long and earnestly through the imperfect and by no means achromatic lens. Enough. I will think of something else. I will think of nothing at all——

Stay. There was a sound at last; a light footfall.

A hare races towards us through the ferns, her great bright eyes full of terror, her ears aloft to catch some sound behind. She sees us, turns short, and vanishes into the gloom. The mare pricks up her ears too, listens, and looks: but not the way the hare has gone. There is something more coming; I can trust the finer sense of the horse, to which (and no wonder) the Middle Age attributed the power of seeing ghosts and fairies impalpable to man's gross eyes. Beside, that hare was not travelling in search of food. She was not loping along, looking around her right and left; but galloping steadily. She has been frightened; she has been put up: but what has put her up? And there, far away among the fir-stems, rings the shriek of a startled blackbird. What has put him up?

That, old mare, at sight whereof your wise eyes widen till they are ready to burst, and your ears are first shot forward towards your nose, and then laid back with vicious intent. Stand still, old woman! Do you think still, after fifteen winters, that you can catch a fox?

A fox it is indeed; a great dog-fox, as red as the fir-stems between which he glides. And yet his legs are black with fresh peat-stains. He is a hunted fox: but he has not been up long.

The mare stands like a statue: but I can feel her trembling between my knees. Positively he does not see us. He sits down in the middle of a ride, turns his great ears right and left, and then scratches one of them with his hind foot, seemingly to make it hear the better. Now he is up again and on.

Beneath yon firs, some hundred yards away, standeth, or rather lieth, for it is on dead flat ground, the famous castle of Malepartus, which beheld the base murder of Lampe the hare, and many a seely soul beside. I

know it well; a patch of sand-heaps, mingled with
great holes, amid the twining fir-roots; ancient home
of the last of the wild beasts. And thither, unto
Malepartus safe and strong, trots Reinecke, where he
hopes to be snug among the labyrinthine windings, and
innumerable starting-holes, as the old apologue has it,
of his ballium, covert-way, and donjon keep. Full
blown in self-satisfaction he trots, lifting his toes deli-
cately, and carrying his brush aloft, as full of cunning
and conceit as that world-famous ancestor of his, whose
deeds of unchivalry were the delight, if not the model,
of knight and kaiser, lady and burgher, in the Middle
Age.

Suddenly he halts at the great gate of Malepartus;
examines it with his nose; goes on to a postern; exa-
mines that also, and then another, and another; while
I perceive afar, projecting from every cave's mouth, the
red and green end of a new fir-faggot. Ah, Reinecke!
fallen is thy conceit, and fallen thy tail therewith. Thou
hast worse foes to deal with than Bruin the bear, or
Isegrim the wolf, or any foolish brute whom thy great
ancestor outwitted. Man the many-counselled has been
beforehand with thee; and the earths are stopped.

One moment he sits down to meditate, and scratches
those trusty counsellors, his ears, as if he would tear
them off, 'revolving swift thoughts in a crafty mind.'

He has settled it now. He is up and off—and at

what a pace! Out of the way, Fauns and Hamadryads, if any be left in the forest. What a pace! And with what a grace beside!

Oh Reinecke, beautiful thou art, of a surety, in spite of thy great naughtiness. Art thou some fallen spirit, doomed to be hunted for thy sins in this life, and in some future life rewarded for thy swiftness, and grace, and cunning, by being made a very messenger of the immortals? Who knows? Not I.

I am rising fast to Pistol's vein. Shall I ejaculate? Shall I notify? Shall I waken the echoes? Shall I break the grand silence by that scream which the vulgar view-halloo call?

It is needless; for louder and louder every moment swells up a sound which makes my heart leap into my mouth, and my mare into the air.

Music? Well-beloved soul of Hullah, would that thou wert here this day, and not in St. Martin's Hall, to hear that chorus, as it pours round the fir-stems, rings against the roof above, shatters up into a hundred echoes, till the air is live with sound! You love madrigals, and whatever Weekes, or Wilbye, or Orlando Gibbons sang of old. So do I. Theirs is music fit for men: worthy of the age of heroes, of Drake and Raleigh, Spenser and Shakspeare: but oh that you could hear this madrigal! If you must have 'four parts,' then there they are. Deeped-mouthed bass, rolling along the ground; rich joyful tenor; wild wistful alto; and leaping up here and there above the throng of sounds, delicate treble shrieks and trills of trembling joy. I know not whether you can fit it into your laws of music, any more than you can the song of that Ariel sprite who dwells in the Eolian harp, or the roar of the waves on the rock, or

> 'Myriads of rivulets hurrying through the lawn,
> And murmur of innumerable bees.'

But music it is. A madrigal? Rather a whole opera of Der Freischutz—dæmoniac element and all— to judge by those red lips, fierce eyes, wild, hungry voices; and such as should make Reinecke, had he strong æsthetic sympathies, well content to be hunted from his cradle to his grave, that such sweet sounds might by him enrich the air. Heroes of old were glad to die, if but some 'vates sacer' would sing their fame in worthy strains: and shalt not thou too be glad, Reinecke? Content thyself with thy fate. Music soothes care; let it soothe thine, as thou runnest for thy life; thou shalt have enough of it in the next hour. For as the Etruscans (says Athenæus) were so luxurious that they used to flog their slaves to the sound of the flute, so shall luxurious Chanter and Challenger, Sweetlips and Melody, eat thee to the sound of rich organpipes, that so thou mayest,

> ' Like that old fabled swan, in music die.

And now appear, dim at first and distant, but brightening and nearing fast, many a right good fellow and many a right good horse. I know three out of four of them, their private histories, the private histories of their horses: and could tell you many a good story of them: but shall not, being an English gentleman, and not an American littérateur. They may not all be very clever, or very learned, or very anything except gallant men; but they are all good enough company for me, or anyone; and each has his own specialité, for which I like him. That huntsman I have known for fifteen years, and sat many an hour beside his father's death-bed. I am godfather to that whip's child. I have seen the servants of the hunt, as I have the hounds, grow up round me for two generations, and I feel for them as old friends; and like to look into their brave, honest, weather-beaten faces. That red coat there, I knew him when he was a schoolboy; and now he is a captain in the Guards, and won his Victoria Cross at Inkermann: that bright green coat is the best farmer, as well as the hardest rider, for many a mile round; one who plays, as he works, with all his might, and might have been a beau sabreur and colonel of dragoons. So might that black coat, who now brews good beer, and stands up for the poor at the Board of Guardians, and rides, like the green coat, as well as he works. That other black coat is a county banker; but

he knows more of the fox than the fox knows of him-
self, and where the hounds' are, there will he be this
day. That red coat has hunted kangaroo in Australia:
that one, as clever and good as he is brave and simple,
has stood by Napier's side in many an Indian fight:
that one won his Victoria at Delhi, and was cut up at
Lucknow, with more than twenty wounds: that one
has—but what matter to you who each man is?
Enough that each can tell one a good story, welcome
one cheerfully, and give one out here, in the wild
forest, the wholesome feeling of being at home among
friends.

There is music, again, if you will listen, in the soft
tread of these hundred horse-hoofs upon the spongy
vegetable soil. They are trotting now in 'common
time.' You may hear the whole Croats' March (the
finest trotting march in the world) played by those iron
heels; the time, as it does in the Croats' March, break-
ing now and then, plunging, jingling, struggling through
heavy ground, bursting for a moment into a jubilant
canter as it reaches a sound spot.

The hounds feather a moment round Malepartus,
puzzled by the windings of Reinecke's footsteps. You
can hear the flap and snort of the dogs' nostrils as they
canter round; and one likes it. It is exciting: but why
—who can tell?

What beautiful creatures they are, too! Next to a

Greek statue (I mean a real old Greek one; for I am a thoroughly anti-preraphaelite benighted pagan heathen in taste, and intend some day to get up a Cinque-Cento Club, for the total abolition of Gothic art)—next to a Greek statue, I say, I know few such combinations of grace and strength as in a fine foxhound. It is the beauty of the Theseus—light and yet massive; and light not in spite of its masses, but on account of the perfect disposition of them. I do not care for grace in man, woman, or animal, which is obtained (as in the old German painters) at the expense of honest flesh and blood. It may be all very pure, and unearthly, and saintly, and what not; but it is not healthy; and, therefore, it is not really High Art, let it call itself such as much as it likes. The highest art must be that in which the outward is the most perfect symbol of the inward; and, therefore, a healthy soul can be only exprest by a healthy body; and starved limbs and a hydrocephalous forehead must be either taken as incorrect symbols of spiritual excellence, or as—what they were really meant for—symbols of certain spiritual diseases which were in the Middle Age considered as ecclesiastical graces and virtues. Wherefore I like pagan and naturalist art; consider Titian and Correggio as unappreciated geniuses, whose excellences the world will in some saner mood rediscover; hold, in direct opposition to Rio, that Rafaelle improved steadily all his life through, and that his noblest works are not his somewhat simpering Madonnas and somewhat impish Bambinos (very lovely though they are), but his great, coarse, naturalist, Protestant cartoons, which (with Andrea Mantegna's Heathen Triumph) Cromwell saved for the British nation. Probably no one will agree with all this for the next quarter of a century: but after that I have hopes. The world will grow tired of pretending to admire Manichæan pictures in an age of natural science; and Art will let the dead bury their dead, and beginning again where Michael Angelo and Rafaelle left off, work forward into a nobler, truer, freer, and more divine school than the world has yet seen—at least, so I hope.

And all this has grown out of those foxhounds. Why not? Theirs is the sort of form which expresses to me what I want Art to express—Nature not limited, but developed, by high civilization. The old savage ideal of beauty was the lion, type of mere massive force. That was succeeded by an over-civilized ideal, say the fawn, type of delicate grace. By cunning breeding and choosing, through long centuries, man has combined both, and has created the foxhound, lion and fawn in one; just as he might create noble human beings; did he take half as much trouble about politics (in the true old sense of the word) as he does about fowls. Look at that old hound, who stands doubtful,

looking up at his master for advice. Look at the
severity, delicacy, lightness of every curve. His head
is finer than a deer's; his hind legs tense as steel
springs; his fore-legs straight as arrows: and yet see
the depth of chest, the sweep of loin, the breadth of
paw, the mass of arm and thigh; and if you have an
eye for form, look at the absolute majesty of his atti-
tude at this moment. Majesty is the only word for it
If he were six feet high, instead of twenty-three inches,
with what animal on earth could you compare him?
Is it not a joy to see such a thing alive? It is to me,
at least. I should like to have one in my study all
day long, as I would have a statue or a picture; and
when Mr. Morrell gave (as they say) two hundred
guineas for Hercules alone, I believe the dog was well
worth the money, only to look at. But I am a minute
philosopher.

I cap them on to the spot at which Reinecke dis-
appeared. Old Virginal's stern flourishes; instantly
her pace quickens. One whimper, and she is away full-
mouthed through the wood, and the pack after her:
but not I.

I am not going with them. My hunting days are
over. Let it suffice that I have, in the days of my
vanity, 'drank delight of battle with my peers, far
on the ringing plains' of many a county, grass and
forest, down and vale. No, my gallant friends. You

K

know that I could ride, if I chose ; and I am vain
enough to be glad that you know it. But useless are
your coaxings, solicitations, wavings of honest right
hands. 'Life,' as my friend Tom Brown says, 'is
not all beer and skittles ;' it is past two now, and I
have four old women to read to at three, and an old
man to bury at four; and I think, on the whole, that
you will respect me the more for going home and
doing my duty. That I should like to see this fox
fairly killed, or even fairly lost, I deny not. That I
should like it as much as I can like any earthly and
outward thing, I deny not. But sugar to one's bread
and butter is not good; and if my winter-garden
represent the bread and butter, then will fox-hunting
stand to it in the relation of superfluous and unwhole-
some sugar : so farewell ; and long may your noble
sport prosper—' the image of war with only half its
danger,' to train you and your sons after, into gallant
soldiers—full of

'The reason firm, the temperate will,
Endurance, foresight, strength and skill.'

So homeward I go through a labyrinth of fir-stems
and, what is worse, fir-stumps, which need both my
eyes and my horse's at every moment; and woe to the
' anchorite,' as old Bunbury names him, who carries his
nose in the air, and his fore feet well under him. Woe

to the self-willed or hard-hided horse who cannot take
the slightest hint of the heel, and wince hind legs or
fore out of the way of those jagged points which lie in
wait for him. Woe, in fact, to all who are clumsy or
cowardly, or in anywise not 'masters of the situation.'

Pleasant riding it is, though, if you dare look any-
where but over your horse's nose, under the dark roof,
between the red fir-pillars, in that rich subdued light.
Now I plunge into a gloomy dell, wherein is no tink-
ling rivulet, ever pure; but instead a bog, hewn out
into a chess-board of squares, parted by deep narrow
ditches some twenty feet apart. Blundering among the
stems I go, fetlock-deep in peat, and jumping at every
third stride one of the said uncanny gripes, half hidden
in long hassock grass. Oh *Aira cæspitosa*, most stately
and most variable of British grasses, why will you
always grow where you are not wanted? Through you
the mare all but left her hind legs in that last gripe.
Through you a red-coat ahead of me, avoiding one of
your hassocks, jumped with his horse's nose full butt
against a fir-stem, and stopped,

> ' As one that is struck dead
> By lightning, ere he falls,'

as we shall soon, in spite of the mare's cleverness.
Would we were out of this!

Out of it we shall be soon. I see daylight ahead at

last, bright between the dark stems. Up a steep slope, and over a bank which is not very big, but being composed of loose gravel and peat mould, gives down with me, nearly sending me head over heels in the heather, and leaving me a sheer gap to scramble through, and out on the open moor.

Grand old moor! stretching your brown flats right away toward Windsor for many a mile.—Far to our right is the new Wellington College, looking stately enough here all alone in the wilderness, in spite of its two ugly towers and pinched waist. Close over me is the long fir-fringed ride of Easthampstead, ending suddenly in Cæsar's camp; and hounds and huntsmen are already far ahead, and racing up the Roman road, which the clods of these parts, unable to give a better account of it, call the Devil's Highway.

Racing indeed; for as Reinecke gallops up the narrow heather-fringed pathway, he brushes off his scent upon the twigs at every stride; and the hounds race after him, showing no head indeed, and keeping, for convenience, in one long line upon the track: but going heads up, sterns down, at a pace which no horse can follow.—I only hope they may not overrun the scent.

They have overrun it; halt, and put their heads down a moment. But with one swift cast in full gallop they have hit it off again, fifty yards away in the heather, long ere the horsemen are up to them; for those hounds can hunt a fox because they are not hunted themselves, and so have learnt to trust themselves, and act for themselves; as boys should learn at school, even at the risk of a mistake or two. Now they are showing head indeed, down a half-cleared valley, and over a few ineffectual turnips withering in the peat, a patch of growing civilization in the heart of the wilderness; and then over the brook, while I turn slowly away, through a green wilderness of self-sown firs.

There they stand in thousands, the sturdy Scots, colonizing the desert in spite of frost, and gales, and barrenness; and clustering together, too, as Scotsmen always do abroad, little and big, every one under his neighbour's lee, according to the good old proverb of their native land, 'Caw me, and I'll caw thee.'

I respect them, those Scotch firs. I delight in their forms, from James the First's gnarled giants up in Bramshill Park—the only place in England where a painter can learn what Scotch firs are—down to the little green pyramids which stand up out of the heather, triumphant over tyranny, and the strange woes of an untoward youth. Seven years on an average have most of them spent in ineffectual efforts to become a foot high. Nibbled off by hares, trodden down by cattle, cut down by turf-parers, seeing hundreds of their brethren cut up and carried off in the turf-fuel, they are as gnarled and stubbed near

the ground as an old thorn-bush in a pasture. But
they have conquered at last, and are growing away,
eighteen inches a year, with fair green brushes silver-
tipt, reclothing the wilderness with a vegetation which
it has not seen for—how many thousand years?

No man can tell. For when last the Scotch fir was
indigenous to England, and, mixed with the larch,
stretched in one vast forest from Norfolk into Wales,
England was not as it is now. Snowdon was, it may
be, fifteen thousand feet in height, and from the edges
of its glaciers the marmot and the musk ox, the elk
and the bear, wandered down into the Lowlands, and
the hyena and the lion dwelt in those caves where fox
and badger only now abide. And how did the Scotch
fir die out? Did the whole land sink slowly from its
sub-Alpine elevation into a warmer climate below? Or
was it never raised at all? Did some change of the
Atlantic sea-floor turn for the first time the warm Gulf
Stream to these shores; and with its soft sea-breezes
melt away the 'Age of Ice,' till glaciers and pines,
marmots and musk oxen, perspired to death, and
vanished for an æon? Who knows? Not I. But
of the fact there can be no doubt. Whether, as we
hold traditionally here, the Scotch fir was re-introduced
by James the First when he built Bramshill for
Raleigh's hapless pet, Henry the Prince, or whatever
may have been the date of their re-introduction, here

they are, and no one can turn them out. In countless thousands the winged seeds float down the south-west gales from the older trees; and every seed which falls takes root in ground which, however unable to bear broad-leaved trees, is ready by long rest for the seeds of the needle-leaved ones. Thousands perish yearly; but the eastward march of the whole, up hill and down dale, is sure and steady as that of Lynceus' Goths in Goethe's Helena :—

'Ein lang und breites Volksgewicht,
Der erste wusste vom letzen nicht.

Der erste fiel, der zweite stand,
Des dritten Lanze war zur Hand,
Ein jeder hundertfach gestärkt;
Erschlagene Tausend unbemerkt——

—till, as you stand upon some eminence, you see, stretching to the eastward of each tract of older trees, a long cloud of younger ones, like a green comet's tail —I wish their substance was as yielding this day. Truly beautiful—grand indeed to me it is—to see young live Nature thus carrying on a great savage process in the heart of this old and seemingly all-artificial English land; and reproducing here, as surely as in the Australian bush, a native forest, careless of mankind. Still, I wish it were easier to ride through. Stiff are those Scotchmen, and close and stout they stand by each other, and claw at you as you twist through them, the biggest aiming at your head, or even worse, at your knees; while the middle-sized slip their brushes between your thigh and the saddle, and the little babies tickle your horse's stomach, or twine about his fore-feet. Whish—whish; we are enveloped in what seems an atmosphere of scrubbing-brushes. Fain would I shut my eyes: but dare not, or I shall ride against a tree. Whish—whish; alas for the horse which cannot wind and turn like a hare! Plunge—stagger. What is this? A broad line of ruts; perhaps some Celtic trackway, two thousand years old, now matted over with firs; dangerous enough out on the open moor, when only masked by a line of higher and darker heath: but doubly dangerous now when masked by dark undergrowth. You must find your own way here, mare. I will positively have nothing to do with it. I disclaim all responsibility. There are the reins on your neck; do what you will, only do something—and if you can, get forward, and not back.

There is daylight at last, and fresh air. I trot contemptuously through the advanced skirmishers of the Scotch invading army; and watch my friends some mile and a half off, who have threaded a practicable trackway through a long dreary yellow bog, too wet for firs to root in, and are away in 'a streamer.' Now a streamer is produced in this wise. There is but one possible gap in a bank, one possible ford in a brook;

one possible path in a cover; and as each man has to wait till the man before him gets through, and then gallops on, each man loses twenty yards or more on the man before him: wherefore, by all laws of known arithmetic, if ten men tail through a gap, then will the last of the ten find himself two hundred yards behind the foremost, which process several times repeated, produces the phenomenon called a streamer, viz. twenty men galloping absurdly as hard as they can, in a line half a mile long, and in humours which are celestial in the few foremost, contented in the central, and gradually becoming darker in the hindmost; till in the last man they assume a hue altogether Tartarean. Farewell, brave gentlemen! I watch, half sadly, half self-contented, the red coats scattered like sparks of fire over hill and dale, and turn slowly homeward, to visit my old women.

I pass through a gateway, out upon a village green, planted with rows of oaks, surrounded by trim sunny cottages, a pleasant oasis in the middle of the wilderness. Across the village cricket-ground—we are great cricketers in these parts, and long may the good old game live among us; and then up another hollow lane, which leads between damp shaughs and copses toward the further moor.

Curious things to a minute philosopher are these same hollow lanes. They set him on archæological

questions, more than he can solve; and I meditate as I
go, how many centuries it took to saw through the warm
sandbanks this dyke ten feet deep, up which he trots,
with the oak boughs meeting over his head. Was it
ever worth men's while to dig out the soil? Surely
not. The old method must have been, to remove the
softer upper spit, till they got to tolerably hard ground;
and then, Macadam's metal being as yet unknown, the
rains and the wheels of generations sawed it gradually
deeper and deeper, till this road-ditch was formed. But
it must have taken centuries to do it. Many of these
hollow lanes, especially those on flat ground, must be
as old or older than the Conquest. In Devonshire I am
sure that they are. But there many of them, one sus-
pects, were made not of malice, but of cowardice pre-
pense. Your indigenous Celt was, one fears, a sneaking
animal, and liked to keep when he could under cover of
banks and hill-sides; while your bold Roman made his
raised roads straight over hill and dale, as 'ridge-ways'
from which, as from an eagle's eyrie, he could survey
the conquered lowlands far and wide. It marks strongly
the difference between the two races, that difference
between the Roman paved road with its established
common way for all passengers, its regular stations and
milestones, and the Celtic trackway winding irresolutely
along in innumerable ruts, parting to meet again, as if
each savage (for they were little better) had taken his

own fresh path when he found the next line of ruts too heavy for his cattle. Around the spurs of Dartmoor I have seen many ancient roads, some of them long disused, which could have been hollowed out for no other purpose but that of concealment.

So I go slowly up the hill, till the valley lies beneath me like a long green garden between its two banks of brown moor; and on through a cheerful little green, with red brick cottages scattered all round, each with its large neat garden, and beehives, and pigs and geese, and turf-stack, and clipt yews and hollies before the door, and rosy dark-eyed children, and all the simple healthy comforts of a wild 'heth-cropper's' home. When he can, the good man of the house works at farm labour, or cuts his own turf; and when work is scarce, he cuts copses and makes heath-brooms, and does a little poaching. True, he seldom goes to church, save to be christened, married, or buried: but he equally seldom gets drunk. For church and public stand together two miles off; so that social wants sometimes bring their own compensations with them, and there are two sides to every question.

Hark! A faint, dreary hollo off the moor above. And then another, and another. My friends may trust it; for the clod of these parts delights in the chase like any bare-legged Paddy, and casts away flail and fork wildly, to run, shout, assist, and interfere in all possible ways, out of pure love. The descendant of many generations of broom-squires and deer-stealers, the instinct of sport is strong within him still, though no more of the king's deer are to be shot in the winter turnip-fields, or worse, caught by an apple-baited hook hung from an orchard bough. He now limits his aspirations to hares and pheasants, and too probably once in his life, ' hits the keeper into the river,' and reconsiders himself for a while after over a crank in Winchester gaol. Well, he has his faults; and I have mine. But he is a thorough good fellow nevertheless; quite as good as I: civil, contented, industrious, and often very handsome; and a far shrewder fellow too—owing to his dash of wild forest blood, from gipsy, highwayman, and what not—than his bullet-headed and flaxen-polled cousin, the pure South-Saxon of the Chalk-downs. Dark-haired he is, ruddy, and tall of bone; swaggering in his youth; but when he grows old, a thorough gentleman, reserved, stately, and courteous as a prince. Sixteen years have I lived with him hail fellow well met, and never yet had a rude word or action from him.

With him I have cast in my lot, to live and die, and be buried by his side; and to him I go home contented, to look after his petty interests, cares, sorrows— Petty, truly—seeing that they include the whole primal mysteries of life—Food, raiment, and work to earn them withal; love and marriage, birth and death, right doing and wrong doing, 'Schicksal und eigene Schuld;' and all those commonplaces of humanity which in the eyes of a minute philosopher are most divine, because they are most commonplace—catholic as the sunshine and the rain which come down from the Heavenly Father, alike upon the evil and the good. As for doing fine things, my friend, with you, I have learnt to believe that I am not set to do fine things, simply because I am not able to do them; and as for seeing fine things, with you, I have learnt to see the sight— as well as to try to do the duty—which lies nearest me; and to comfort myself with the fancy that if I make good use of my eyes and brain in this life, I shall see— if it be of any use to me—all the fine things, or perhaps finer still, in the life to come. But if not—what matter? In any life, in any state, however simple or humble, there will be always sufficient to occupy a Minute Philosopher; and if a man be busy, and busy about his duty, what more does he require, for time or for eternity?

V.

FROM OCEAN TO SEA.

V.

FROM OCEAN TO SEA.

The point from which to start, in order best to appreciate the change from ocean to sea, is perhaps Biarritz. The point at which to stop is Cette. And the change is important. Between the two points races are changed, climates are changed, scenery is changed, the very plants under your feet are changed, from a Western to an Eastern type. You pass from the wild Atlantic into the heart of the Roman Empire—from the influences which formed the discoverers of the New World, to those which formed the civilizers of the Old. Gascony, not only in its scenery, but in its very legends, reminds you of Devon and Cornwall; Languedoc of Greece and Palestine.

In the sea, as was to be expected, the change is even more complete. From Biarritz to Cette, you pass from poor Edward Forbes's Atlantic to his Mediterranean centre of creation. In plain English and fact, whether

K

you agree with his theory or not, you pass from the region of respectable whales, herrings, and salmon, to that of tunnies, sciænas, dorados, and all the gorgons, hydras, and chimæras dire, which are said to grace the fish-markets of Barcelona or Marseilles.

But to this assertion, as to most concerning nature, there are exceptions. Mediterranean fishes slip out of the Straits of Gibraltar, and up the coast of Portugal, and, once in the Bay of Biscay, find the feeding good and the wind against them, and stay there.

So it befalls, that at worthy M. Gardère's hotel at Biarritz (he has seen service in England, and knows our English ways), you may have at dinner, day after day, salmon, louvine, shad, sardine, dorado, tunny. The first is unknown to the Mediterranean; for Fluellen mistook when he said that there were salmons in Macedon, as well as Monmouth; the louvine is none other than the nasty bass, or sea-perch of the Atlantic; the shad (extinct in these islands, save in the Severn) is a gigantic herring which comes up rivers to spawn; a fish common (with slight differences) to both sides of the North Atlantic; while the sardine, the dorado, and the tunny (whether he be the true tunny or the Ala-longa) are Mediterranean fish.

The whale fishery of these shores is long extinct. The Biscayan whale was supposed to be extinct likewise. But like the ibex, and some other animals

which man has ceased to hunt, because he fancies that
he has killed them all, they seem inclined to reappear.
For in 1854 one was washed ashore near St. Jean de
Luz, at news whereof Eschricht, the great Danish natu-
ralist, travelled night and day from Copenhagen, and
secured the skeleton of the new-old monster.

But during the latter part of the Middle Ages, and
on—if I recollect aright—into the seventeenth century,
Bayonne, Biarritz, Guettary, and St. Jean de Luz, sent
forth their hardy whale-fishers, who slew all the whales
of the Biscayan seas, and then crossed the Atlantic, to
attack those of the frozen North.

British and American enterprise drove them from the
West coast of the Atlantic; and now their descendants
are content to stay at home and take the sardine-shoals,
and send them in to Bayonne on their daughters' heads.

Pretty enough it was, at least in outward seeming, to
meet a party of those fisher-girls, bare-legged, high-
kilted, lithe as deer, trotting, at a long loping pace, up
the high road toward Bayonne, each with her basket on
her head, as she laughed and sang, and tossed her black
hair, and flashed her brown eyes, full of life and the
enjoyment of life. Pretty enough. And yet who will
blame the rail, which now sends her quickly into
Bayonne—or even her fish without her; and relieves
the fair young maiden from being degraded into a
beast of burden?

Handsome folk are these brown Basques. A mysterious people, who dwell alone, and are not counted among the nations; speaking an unique language, and keeping up unique customs, for which the curious must consult M. Michel's interesting book. There may be a cross of English blood among them, too, about Biarritz and Bayonne; English features there are, plainly to be seen. And whether or not, one accepts the story of the country, that Anglets, near by, is an old English colony left by our Black Prince, it is certain that Bayonne Cathedral was built in part by English architects, and carries the royal arms of England; and every school history will tell us how this corner of France was long in our hands, and was indeed English long before it was properly French. Moorish blood there may be, too, here and there, left behind by those who built the little 'atalaya' or fire-beacon, over the old harbour, to correspond, by its smoke column, with a long line of similar beacons down the Spanish coast. The Basques resemble in look the Southern Welsh—quick-eyed, neat in feature, neat in dress, often, both men and women, beautiful. The men wear a flat Scotch cap of some bright colour, and call it 'berretta.' The women tie a gaudy handkerchief round their heads, and compel one corner to stand forward from behind the ear in a triangle, in proportion to the size and stiffness whereof the lady seems to think herself well dressed. But

the pretty Basque handkerchief will soon give place
to the Parisian bonnet. For every cove among the
rocks is now filled with smart bathing-houses, from
which, in summer, the gay folk of Paris issue in
'costume de bain,' to float about all day on cala-
bashes—having literally no room for the soles of their
feet on land. Then are opened casinos, theatre,
shops, which lie closed all the winter. Then do the
Basque house-owners flee into the moors, and camp
out (it is said) on the hills all night, letting their
rooms for ten francs a night as mere bed-chambers—
for all eating and living is performed in public;
while the dove-coloured oxen, with brown holland
pinafores over their backs, who dawdle in pairs up
and down the long street with their light carts, have
to make way for wondrous equipages from the Bois
de Boulogne.

Not then, for the wise man, is Biarritz a place to
see and to love: but in the winter, when a little
knot of quiet pleasant English hold the place against
all comers, and wander, undisturbed by fashion, about
the quaint little rocks and caves and natural bridges—
and watch tumbling into the sea, before the Biscayan
surges, the trim walks and summer-houses, which
were erected by the municipality in honour of the
Empress and her suite. Yearly they tumble in, and
yearly are renewed, as the soft greensand strata are

graven away, and what must have been once a long promontory becomes a group of fantastic pierced rocks, exactly like those which are immortalized upon the willow-pattern plates.

Owing to this rapid destruction, the rocks of Biarritz are very barren in sea-beasts and sea-weeds. But there is one remarkable exception, where the pools worn in a hard limestone are filled with what seem at first sight beds of china-asters, of all loveliest colours—primrose, sea-green, dove, purple, crimson, pink, ash-grey. They are all prickly sea-eggs (presumably the *Echinus lividus*, which is found in similar places in the west of Ireland), each buried for life in a cup-shaped hole which he has excavated in the rock, and shut in by an overhanging lip of living lime—seemingly a Nullipore coralline. What they do there, what they think of, or what food is brought into their curious grinding-mills by the Atlantic surges which thunder over them twice a day, who can tell? However they form, without doubt, the most beautiful object which I have ever seen in pool or cove.

But the glory of Biarritz, after all, is the moors above, and the view to be seen therefrom. Under blazing blue skies, tempered by soft dappled cloud, for ever sliding from the Atlantic and the Asturias mountains, in a climate soft as milk, and exhilarating withal as wine, one sees far and wide a panorama which, from its variety as well as its beauty, can never weary.

To the north, the long sand-line of the Biscayan shore—the bar of the Adour marked by a cloud of grey spray. Then the dark pine-flats of the Landes, and the towers of Bayonne rising through rich woods. To the eastward lies a high country, furred with woods, broken with glens; a country exactly like Devon, through the heart of which, hidden in such a gorge as that of Dart or Taw, runs the swift stream of the Nive, draining the western Pyrenees. And beyond, to the south-east, in early spring, the Pyrenean snows gleam bright, white clouds above the clouds. As one turns southward, the mountains break down into brown heather-hills, like Scottish grouse moors. The two nearest, and seemingly highest, are the famous Rhune and Bayonette, where lie, to this day, amid the heath and crags, hundreds of unburied bones. For those great hills, skilfully fortified by Soult before the passage of the Bidassoa, were stormed, yard by yard, by Wellington's army in October 1813. That mighty deed must be read in the pages of one who saw it with his own eyes, and fought there with his own noble body, and even nobler spirit. It is not for me to tell of victories, of which Sir William Napier has already told.

Towards that hill, and the Nivelle at its foot, the

land slopes down, still wooded and broken, bounded
by a long sweep of clayey crumbling cliff. The eye
catches the fort of Secoa, at the mouth of the Nivelle—
once Wellington's sea-base for his great French cam-
paign. Then Fontarabia, at the Bidassoa mouth; and
far off, the cove within which lies the fatal citadel
of St. Sebastian; all backed up by the fantastic
mountains of Spain; the four-horned "Quatre Cou-
ronnes," the pyramidal Jaysquivel, and beyond them
again, sloping headlong into the sea, peak after peak,
each one more blue and tender than the one before,
leading the eye on and on for seemingly countless
leagues, till they die away into the ocean horizon and
the boundless west. Not a sail, often for days together,
passes between those mountains and the shore on
which we stand, to break the solitude, and peace,
and vast expanse; and we linger, looking and looking
at we know not what, and find repose in gazing
purposeless into the utter void.

Very unlike France are these Basque uplands; very
like the seaward parts of Devon and Cornwall. Large
oak-copses and boggy meadows fill the glens; while
above, the small fields, with their five-barred gates
(relics of the English occupation) and high furze and
heath-grown banks, make you fancy yourself for a
moment in England. And the illusion is strengthened,
as you see that the heath of the banks is the Goonhilly

heath of the Lizard Point, and that of the bogs the
orange-belled *Erica ciliaris*, which lingers (though rare)
both in Cornwall and in the south of Ireland. But
another glance undeceives you. The wild flowers are
new, saving those cosmopolitan seeds (like nettles and
poppies) which the Romans have carried all over
Europe, and the British are now carrying over the
world. Every sandy bank near the sea is covered with
the creeping stems of a huge reed, which grows in
summer tall enough to make not only high fences,
but fishing-rods. Poverty (though there is none of
what we call poverty in Britain) fills the little walled
court before its cottage with bay trees and standard
figs; while wealth (though there is nothing here of
what we call wealth in Britain) asserts itself uniformly
by great standard magnolias, and rich trailing roses,
in full bloom here in April instead of—as with us—
in July. Both on bank and in bog grow Scorzoneras
(dandelions with sword-shaped leaves) of which there
are none in these isles; and every common is ablaze
with strange and lovely flowers. Each dry spot is
brilliant with the azure flowers of a prostrate Litho-
spermum, so exquisite a plant, that it is a marvel why
we do not see it, as 'spring-bedding,' in every British
garden. The heath is almost hidden, in places, by the
large white flowers and trailing stems of the sage-
leaved Cistus. Delicate purple Ixias, and yet more

delicate Hoop-petticoat Narcissus, spring from the turf.
And here and there among furze and heath, crop out
great pink bunches of the *Daphne Cneorum* of our
gardens, perfuming all the air. Yes, we are indeed
in foreign parts, in the very home of that Atlantic
flora, of which only a few species have reached the
south-west of these isles; and on the limit of another
flora also—of that of Italy and Greece. For as we
descend into the glen, every lane-bank and low
tree is entwined, not with ivy, but with a still
more beautiful evergreen, the Smilax of South-eastern
Europe, with its zigzag stems, and curving heart-
shaped leaves, and hooked thorns; the very oak-scrub
is of species unknown to Britain. And what are
these tall lilies, which fill every glade breast-high with
their sword-like leaves, and spires of white flowers,
lilac-pencilled? They are the classic flower, the
Asphodel of Greece and Grecian song; the Asphodel
through which the ghosts of Homer's heroes strode:
as heroes' ghosts might stride even here.

For here we are on sacred ground. The vegetation
is rank with the blood of gallant invaders, and of no
less gallant patriots. In the words of Campbell's
'Hohenlinden'—

> ' Every turf beneath our feet
> May be a hero's sepulchre.'

That little tarn below has 'bubbled with crimson

foam' when the kings of Europe arose to bring home
the Bourbons, as did the Lake Regillus of old, in the
day when 'the Thirty Cities swore to bring the
Tarquins home.'

Turn to the left, above the tarn, and into the great
Spanish road from Bayonne to the frontier at what
was lately 'La Negresse,' but is now a gay railway
station. Where that station is, was another tarn,
now drained. The road ran between the two. And
that narrow space of two hundred yards, on which
we stand, was for three fearful days the gate of
France.

For on the 10th of December, 1813, Soult, driven
into Bayonne by Wellington's advance, rushed out
again in the early morn, and poured a torrent of
living men down this road, and upwards again towards
the British army which crested that long ridge in
front.

The ridge slopes rapidly away at the back, toward
the lowlands of the Bidassoa; and once thrust from
it, the English army would have been cut in two—
one half driven back upon their sea-base at St. Jean
de Luz: the other half left on the further side of
the Adour.

And this was the gate, which had to be defended
during a three days' battle. That long copse which
overhangs the road is the famous wood, which was

taken and retaken many times. Yon house above it, embowered in trees, is the 'Mayor's house,' in which Sir John Hope was so nearly captured by the French. Somewhere behind the lane where we came down was the battery which blasted off our troops as they ran up from the lowlands behind, to support their fellows.

Of the details of the fight you must read in Napier's 'Peninsular War,' and in Mr. Gleig's 'Subaltern.' They are not to be described by one who never saw a battle, great or small.

And now, if you choose to start upon your journey from the ocean to the sea, you will take the railroad here, and run five miles through the battle-fields into Bayonne, the quaint old fortress city, girdled with a labyrinth of walls, and turf-dykes, and outside them meadows as rich, and trees as stately, as if war had never swept across the land. You may stop, if you will, to look at the tall Spanish houses, with their piazzas and jalousies, and the motley populace, French, Basques, Spaniards, Jews; and, most worth seeing of all, the lovely ladies of Bayonne, who swarm out when the sun goes down, for air and military music. You may try to find (in which you will probably fail) the arms of England in the roof of the ugly old cathedral; you may wander over the bridges which join the three quarters of the city (for the Adour and

the Nive meet within the walls), and probably lose
your way—a slight matter among folk who, if you
will but take off your hat, call them Monsieur,
apologize for the trouble you are giving, begin the
laugh at your own stupidity, and compliment them
on their city and their fair ladies, will be delighted
to walk a mile out of their own way to show you
yours. You will gaze up at the rock-rooted citadel
from whence, in the small hours of April 14, 1813,
after peace was agreed on, but unhappily not declared
(for Napier has fully exculpated the French Generals),
three thousand of Thouvenot's men burst forth against
Sir John Hope's unsuspecting besiegers, with a furious
valour which cost the English more than 800 men.

There, in the pine woods on the opposite side, is the
Boucault, where our besieging army lay. Across the
reach below stretched Sir John Hope's famous bridge;
and as you leave Bayonne by rail, you run beneath
the English cemetery, where lie the soldiers (officers
of the Coldstream Guards among them) who fell in
the Frenchman's last struggle to defend his native
land.

But enough of this. I should not have recalled to
mind one of these battles, had they not, one and all,
been as glorious for the French and their great captain
—wearied with long marches, disheartened by the
apathy of their own countrymen, and, as they went on,

overpowered by mere numbers—as they were for our veterans, and Wellington himself.

And now, once through Bayonne, we are in the Pignadas and the Landes.

To form a conception of these famous Landes, it is only necessary to run down by the South-Western Railway, through the moors of Woking or Ascot; spread them out flat, and multiply them to seeming infinity. The same sea of brown heather, broken only by the same dark pignadas, or fir plantations, extends for nigh a hundred miles; and when the traveller northward has lost sight, first of the Spanish mountains, and then of the Pyrenean snows, he seems to be rushing along a brown ocean, without wave or shore. Only, instead of the three heaths of Surrey and Hants (the same species as those of Scotland), larger and richer southern heaths cover the grey sands; and notably the delicate upright spires of the bruyère, or *Erica scoparia,* which grows full six feet high, and furnishes from its roots those 'bruyère' pipes, which British shopkeepers have rechristened 'briar-roots.' Instead, again, of the Scotch firs of Ascot, the pines are all pinasters (miscalled *P. maritima*). Each has the same bent stem, carrying at top, long, ragged, scanty, leaf-tufts, instead of the straight stem and dense short foliage of the sturdier Scotchman; and down each stem runs a long, fresh scar, and at the bottom (in spring at least), hangs a lip of tin, and a neat earthen pipkin, into which distils turpentine as clear as glass. The trees have mostly been planted within the last fifty years, to keep the drifting sands from being blown away. As timber they are about as valuable as those Jersey cow-cabbage stalks, of which the curious will at times make walking-sticks : but as producers of turpentine they have their use, and give employment to the sad, stunted, ill-fed folk, unhealthy for want of water, and barbarous from utter loneliness, whose only employment, in old times, was the keeping ragged flocks about the moors. Few and far between the natives may be seen from the railway, seemingly hung high in air, till on nearer approach you find them to be stalking along on stilts, or standing knitting on the same, a sheepskin over their shoulders, an umbrella strapped to their side, and, stuck into the small of the back, a long crutch, which serves, when resting, as a third wooden leg.

So run on the Landes, mile after mile, station after station, varied only by an occasional stunted cork tree, or a starved field of barley or maize. But the railroad is bringing to them, as elsewhere, labour, civilization, agricultural improvement. Pretty villages, orchards, gardens, are springing up round the lonely 'gares.' The late Emperor helped forward, it is said, new pine plantations, and sundry schemes for reclaiming the waste. Arcachon, on a pine-fringed lagoon of the Atlantic, has great artificial ponds for oyster breeding, and is rising into a gay watering-place, with a distinguished scientific society. Nay, more : it saw a few years since an international exposition of fish, and fish-culture, and fishing-tackle, and all things connected with the fisheries, not only of Europe, but of America likewise. Heaven speed the plan ; and restore thereby oysters to our shores, and shad and salmon to the rivers both of Western Europe and Eastern North America.

As for the cause of the Landes, it may be easily divined, by the help of a map and of common sense.

The Gironde and the Adour carry to the sea the drainage of nearly a third of France, including almost all the rain which falls on the north side of the Pyrenees. What has become of all the sand and mud which has been swept in the course of ages down their channels? What has become—a very small part, be it recollected, of the whole amount—of all the rock which has been removed by rain and thunder, frost and snow, in the process of scooping out the deep valleys of the Pyrenees ? Out of that one crack, which men call the Val d'Ossan, stone has been swept enough to form a considerable island. Where is it all ? In these Landes. Carried down year by year to the Atlantic, it has been driven back again, year by year, by the fierce gales of the Bay of Biscay, and rolled up into banks and dunes of loose sand, till it has filled up what was once a broad estuary, 140 miles across and perhaps 70 miles in depth. Upheaved it may have been also, slowly, from the sea, for recent sea-shells are found as far inland as Dax; and thus the whole upper end of the Bay of Biscay has transformed itself during the lapse of, it may be, countless ages, into a desolate wilderness.

It is at Dax that we leave the main line, and instead of running north for Bordeaux and the land of clarets, turn south-east to Orthez and Pau, and the Gaves, and the Pyrenees.

And now we pass through ragged uplands, woody and moorish, with the long yellow maize-stalks of last year's crop rotting in the swampy glens. For the 'petite culture,' whatever be its advantages, gives no capital or power of combined action for draining wet lands; and the valleys of Gascony and Bearn in the south, as well as great sheets of the Pas de Calais in the north, are in a waterlogged state, equally shocking to the eye of a British farmer, and injurious to the health and to the crops of the peasants.

Soon we strike the Adour, here of the shape and size of a second-class Scotch salmon-stream, with swirling brown pools beneath grey crags, which make one long to try in them the virtues of 'Jock Scott,'

K

'the Butcher,' or the 'Dusty Miller.' And perhaps not without effect; for salmon are there still; and will be more and more as French 'pisciculture' develops itself under Government supervision.

Here we touch again the line of that masterly retreat of Soult's before the superior forces of Wellington, to which Napier has done such ample and deserved justice.

There is Berenz, where the Sixth and Light divisions crossed the Gave, and clambered into the high road up steep ravines; and there is Orthez itself, with the beautiful old Gothic bridge which the French could not blow up, as they did every other bridge on their retreat; and the ruins of that robber den to which Gaston Phœbus, Count of Foix (of whom you may read in Froissart), used to drag his victims; and there overhead, upon the left of the rail and road, is the old Roman camp, and the hill of Orthez, and St. Boes, and the High Church of Baights, the scene of the terrible battle of Orthez.

The Roman camp, then 'open and grassy, with a few trees,' says Napier, is now covered with vineyards. Everywhere the fatal slopes are rich with cultivation, plenty, and peace. God grant they may remain so for ever.

And so, along the Gave de Pau, we run on to Pau, the ancient capital of Bearn; the birthplace of Henri

Quatre, and of Bernadotte, King of Sweden ; where, in the charming old château, restored by Louis Philippe, those who list may see the tortoise which served as the great Henry's cradle ; and believe, if they list also, the tale that that is the real shell.

For in 1793, when the knights of the 'bonnet rouge' and 'carmagnole complete' burst into the castle, to destroy every memorial of hated royalty, the shell among the rest, there chanced—miraculous coincidence —to be in Pau, in the collection of a naturalist, another shell, of the same shape and size. Swiftly and deftly pious hands substituted it for the real relic, leaving it to be battered in pieces and trampled in the mud, while the royal cradle lay perdu for years in the roof of a house, to reappear duly at the Restoration of the Bourbons.

Of Pau I shall say nothing. It would be real impertinence in one who only spent three days in it, to describe a city which is known to all Europe ; which is a permanent English colony, and boasts of one, and sometimes two, packs of English fox-hounds. But this I may be allowed to say. That of all delectable spots I have yet seen, Pau is the most delectable. Of all the landscapes which I have beheld, that from the Place Royale is, for variety, richness, and grandeur, the most glorious ; at least as I saw it for the first time.

Beneath the wall of the high terrace are rich

meadows, vocal with frogs rejoicing in the rain, and expressing their joy, not in the sober monotone of our English frogs, but each according to his kind; one bellowing, the next barking, the next cawing, and the next (probably the little green Hylas, who has come down out of the trees to breed) quacking in treble like a tiny drake. The bark (I suspect) is that of the gorgeous edible frog; and so suspect the young recruits who lounge upon the wall, and look down wistfully, longing, I presume, to eat him. And quite right they are; for he (at least his thigh) is exceeding good to eat, tenderer and sweeter than any spring chicken.

Beyond the meadow, among the poplars, the broad Gave murmurs on over shingly shallows, between aspen-fringed islets, grey with the melting snows; and beyond her again rise broken wooded hills, dotted with handsome houses; and beyond them a veil of mist and rain.

On a sudden that veil lifts; and five-and-twenty miles away, beneath the black edge of the cloud, against the clear blue sky, stands out the whole snow-range of the Pyrenees; and in the midst, exactly opposite, filling up a vast gap which is the Val d'Ossan, the huge cone, still snowy white, of the Pic du Midi.

He who is conversant with theatres will be unable to overlook the seeming art—and even artifice—of such an effect. The clouds lift like a drop-scene; the mountains are so utterly unlike any natural object in the north, that for the moment one fancies them painted and not real; the Pic du Midi stands so exactly where it ought, and is yet so fantastic and unexpected in its shape, that an artist seems to have put it there.

But he who knows nothing, and cares less, about theatres and their sham glories, and sees for the first time in his life the eternal snows of which he has read since childhood, draws his breath deeply, and stands astounded, whispering to himself that God is great.

One hint more, ere we pass on from Pau. Here, at least in spring time, of all places in Europe, may a man feed his ears with song of birds. The copses by the Gave, the public walks and woods (wherein English prejudices have happily protected what is elsewhere shot down as game, even to the poor little cock-robins whose corpses lie by dozens in too many French markets), are filled with all our English birds of passage, finding their way northwards from Morocco and Algiers; and with our English nightingales, black-caps, willow-wrens, and whitethroats, are other song-sters which never find their way to these isles, for which you must consult the pages of Mr. Gould or Mr. Bree—and chief among them the dark Orpheus, and the yellow Hippolais, surpassing the blackcap, and almost equalling the nightingale, for richness and variety of song—the polyglot warbler which penetrates,

in summer, as far north as the shores of the British
Channel, and there stops short, scared by the twenty
miles of sea, after a land journey—and by night, too, as
all the warblers journey—from Africa.

At Pau, the railroad ended when I was there; and
who would go eastward had to take carriage, and go by
the excellent road (all public roads in the south of
France are excellent, and equal to our best English
roads) over the high Landes to Tarbes; and on again
over fresh Landes to Montrejean; and thence by rail-
way to Toulouse.

They are very dreary, these high flat uplands, from
which innumerable streams pour down to swell the
Adour and the Garonne ; and as one rolls along, listen-
ing to the eternal tinkle of the horse-bells, only two
roadside objects are particularly worthy of notice.   First,
the cultivation, spreading rapidly since the Revolution,
over what was open moor; and next the great natural
parks which one traverses here and there ; the remnants
of those forests which were once sacred to the seigneurs
and their field sports.   The seigneurs are gone now, and
the game with them ; and the forests are almost gone—
so ruinate, indeed, by the peasantry, that the Govern-
ment (I believe) has interfered to stop a destruction of
timber, which involves the destruction both of fire-wood
and of the annual fall of rain.   But the trees which
remain, whether in forest or in homestead, are sadly

'mangled. The winters are sharp in these high uplands, and firing scarce; and the country method of obtaining it is to send a woman up a tree, where she hacks off, with feeble arms and feeble tools, boughs half-way out from the stem, disfiguring, and in time destroying by letting the wet enter, splendid southern oaks, chestnuts, and walnuts. Painful and hideous, to an eye accustomed to British parks, are the forms of these once noble trees.

Suddenly we descend a brow into the Vale of Tarbes: a good land and large; a labyrinth of clear streams, water-meadows, cherry-orchards, and crops of every kind, and in the midst the pleasant old city, with its once famous University. Of Tarbes, you may read in the pages of Froissart—or, if you prefer a later authority, in those of Dumas, ' Trois Mousquetaires ;' for this is the native land of the immortal Ulysses of Gascony, the Chevalier d'Artagnan.

There you may see, to your surprise, not only gentlemen, but ladies, taking their pleasure on horseback after the English fashion; for there is close by a great ' haras,' or Government establishment for horse-breeding. You may watch the quaint dresses in the market-place ; you may rest, as Froissart rested of old, in a ' right pleasant inn ;' you may eat of the delicious cookery which is to be found, even in remote towns, throughout the south of France, and even—if you dare—of

'Coquilles aux Champignons.' You may sit out after dinner in that delicious climate, listening to the rush of the clear Adour through streets, and yards, and culverts; for the city, like Romsey, or Salisbury, is built over many streams. You may watch the Pyrenees changing from white to rose, from rose to lead colour, and then dying away into the night—for twilight there is little or none, here in the far south.

> 'The sun's rim dips, the stars rush out,
> At one stride comes the dark.'

And soon from street to street you hear the 'clarion' of the garrison, that singularly wild and sweet trumpet-call which sends French soldiers to their beds. And at that the whole populace swarms out, rich and poor, and listens entranced beneath the trees in the Place Maubourguet, as if they had never heard it before; with an order and a sobriety, and a good humour, and a bowing to each other, and asking and giving of cigar-lights between men of every class—and a little quiet modest love-making on the outskirts of the crowd, which is very pleasant to behold. And when the music is silent, and the people go off suddenly, silently, and soberly withal (for there are no drunkards in these parts), to their early beds, you stand and look up into the 'purple night,' as Homer calls it—that southern sky, intensely dark, and yet transparent

withal, through which you seem to look beyond the
stars into the infinite itself, and recollect that beyond
all that, and through all that likewise, there is an
infinite good God who cares for all these simple kindly
folk; and that by Him all their hearts are as well
known, and all their infirmities as mercifully weighed,
as are, you trust, your own.

And so you go to rest, content to say, with the wise
American, ' It takes all sorts to make a world.'

The next morn you rise, to roll on over yet more
weary uplands to Montrejeau, over long miles of
sandy heath, a magnified Aldershott, which during
certain summer months is gay, here and there, like
Aldershott, with the tents of an army at play. But
in spring the desolation is utter, and the loneliest
grouse-moor, and the boggiest burn, are more cheerful
and varied than the Landes of Lannemezan, and the
foul streamlets which have sawn gorges through the
sandy waste.

But all the while, on your right hand, league after
league, ever fading into blue sky behind you, and
growing afresh out of blue sky in front, hangs high in
air the white saw of the Pyrenees. High, I say, in
air, for the land slopes, or seems to slope, down from
you to the mountain range, and all their roots are lost
in a dim sea of purple haze. But shut out the snow
line above, and you will find that the seeming haze

is none, but really a clear and richly varied distance of hills, and woods, and towns, which have become invisible from the contrast of their greens, and greys, and purples, with the glare and dazzle of the spotless snows of spring.

There they stand, one straight continuous jagged wall, of which no one point seems higher than another. From the Pic d'Ossan, by the Mont Perdu and the Maladetta to the Pic de Lart, are peaks past counting— hard clear white against the hard clear blue, and blazing with keen light beneath the high southern sun. Each peak carries its little pet cushion of cloud, hanging motionless a few hundred yards above in the blue sky, a row of them as far as eye can see. But, ever and anon, as afternoon draws on, one of those little clouds, seeming tired of waiting at its post ever since sunrise, loses its temper, boils, swells, settles down on its own private peak, and explodes in a fierce thunderstorm down its own private valley, without discomposing in the least its neighbour cloud-cushions right and left. Faintly the roll of the thunder reaches the ear. Across some great blackness of cloud and cliff, a tiny spark darts down. A long wisp of mist sweeps rapidly toward you across the lowlands, and a momentary brush of cold rain lays the dust. And then the pageant is played out, and the disturbed peak is left clear again in the blue sky for the rest of the day, to gather another cloud-cushion when to-morrow's sun shall rise.

To him who looks, day after day, on this astonishing natural wall, stretching, without visible gap, for nearly three hundred miles, it is easy to see why France not only is, but must be, a different world from Spain. Even human thought cannot, to any useful extent, fly over that great wall of homeless rock and snow. On the other side there must needs be another folk, with another tongue, other manners, other politics, and if not another creed, yet surely with other, and utterly different, conceptions of the universe, and of man's business therein. Railroads may do somewhat. But what of one railroad; or even of two, one on the ocean, one on the sea, two hundred and seventy miles apart? Before French civilization can inform and elevate the Spanish people you must 'plane down the Pyrenees.'

At Montrejean, a pretty town upon a hill which overhangs the Garonne, you find, again, verdure and a railroad; and, turning your back upon the Pyrenees, run down the rich ugly vale of the Garonne, through crops of exceeding richness—wheat, which is reaped in July, to be followed by buckwheat reaped in October; then by green crops to be cut in May, and that again by maize, to be pulled in October, and followed by wheat and the same rotation.

Thus you reach Toulouse, a noble city, of which
it ill befits a passer-through to speak. Volumes have
been written on its antiquities, and volumes on its
history; and all of either that my readers need know,
they will find in Murray's hand-book.

At Toulouse—or rather on leaving it to go eastward
—you become aware that you have passed into a fresh
region. The change has been, of course, gradual: but
it has been concealed from you by passing over the
chilly dreary uplands of Lannemezan. Now you find
yourself at once in Languedoc. You have passed from
the Atlantic region into the Mediterranean; from the
old highlands of the wild Vascones, into those lowlands
of Gallia Narbonensis, reaching from the head-waters
of the Garonne to the mouths of the Rhone, which
were said to be more Italian than Italy itself.

The peculiarity of the district is its gorgeous colour-
ing. Everywhere, over rich plains, you look away to
low craggy banks of limestone, the grey whereof
contrasts strongly with the green of the lowland,
and with the even richer green of the mulberry
orchards; and beyond them again, southward to the
now distant snows of the Pyrenees, and northward to
the orange downs and purple glens of the Cevennes,
all blazing in the blazing sun. Green, grey, orange,
purple, and, in the farthest distance, blue as of the
heaven itself, make the land one vast rainbow, and fit

dwelling-place for its sunny folk, still happy and industrious — once the most cultivated and luxurious people in Europe.

As for their industry, it is hereditary. These lands were, it may be, as richly and carefully tilled in the days of Augustus Cæsar as they are now; or rather, as they were at the end of the eighteenth century. For, since then, the delver and sower — for centuries the slave of the Roman, and, for centuries after, the slave of Teutonic or Saracenic conquerors—has become his own master, and his own landlord; and an impulse has been given to industry, which is shown by trim cottages, gay gardens, and fresh olive orchards, pushed up into glens which in a state of nature would starve a goat.

The special culture of the country—more and more special as we run eastward—is that of the mulberry, the almond, and the olive. Along every hill-side, down every glen, lie orchard-rows of the precious pollards. The mulberries are of richest dark velvet green; the almonds, one glory of rose-colour in early spring, are now of a paler and colder green; the olives (as all the world knows) of a dusty grey, which looks all the more desolate in the pruning time of early spring, when half the boughs of the evergreen are cut out, leaving the trees stripped as by a tempest, and are carried home for fire-wood in the quaint little carts, with their solid creaking wheels, drawn by dove-coloured kine. Very ancient are some of these olives, or rather, olive-groups. For when the tree grows old, it splits, and falls asunder, as do often our pollard willows; the bark heals over on the inside of each fragment, and what was one tree becomes many, springing from a single root, and bearing such signs of exceeding age that one can well believe the country tale, how in the olive grounds around Nismes are still fruiting olives which have furnished oil for the fair Roman dames who cooled themselves in the sacred fountain of Nemausa, in the days of the twelve Cæsars.

Between the pollard rows are everywhere the rows of vines, or of what will be vines when summer comes, but are now black knobbed and gnarled clubs, without a sign of life save here and there one fat green shoot of leaf and tendril bursting forth from the seemingly dead stick.

One who sees that sight may find a new meaning and beauty in the mystic words, 'I am the vine, ye are the branches.' It is not merely the connection between branch and stem, common to all trees; not merely the exhilarating and seemingly inspiring properties of the grape, which made the very heathens look upon it as the sacred and miraculous fruit, the special gift of God; not merely the pruning out of the unfruitful branches, to be burned as fire-wood, or—after the old Roman fashion, which I believe endures still in these parts—buried as manure at the foot of the parent stem; not merely these, but the seeming death of the vine, shorn of all its beauty, its fruitfulness, of every branch and twig which it had borne the year before, and left unsightly and seemingly ruined, to its winter's sleep; and then bursting forth again, by an irresistible inward life, into fresh branches spreading and trailing far and wide, and tossing their golden tendrils to the sun.

This thought, surely—the emblem of the living Church springing from the corpse of the dead Christ, who yet should rise and be alive for evermore—enters into, it may be forms an integral part of, the meaning of, that prophecy of all prophecies.

One ought to look, with something of filial reverence, on the agriculture of the district into which we are penetrating; for it is the parent of our own. From hence, or strictly speaking from the Mediterranean shore beyond us, spread northward and westward through France, Belgium, and Britain, all the tillage which we knew—at least till a hundred years ago— beyond the primæval plan of clearing, or . surface-burning, the forests, growing miserable white crops as long as they would yield, and then letting the land relapse, for twenty years, into miserable pasture. This process (which lingered thirty years ago in remote parts of Devon), and nothing better, seems to have been that change of cultivated lands which Tacitus ascribes to the ancient Germans. Rotation of crops, in any true sense, came to us from Provence and Languedoc; and with it, subsoiling; irrigation; all our artificial grasses, with lucerne at the head of the list; our peas and beans; some of our most important roots; almost all our garden flowers, vegetables, fruits, the fig, the mulberry, the vine—(the olive and the maize came with them from the East, but dared go no further north)—and I know not what more; till we may say, that —saving subsoil-draining, which their climate does not need—the ancestors of these good folks were better farmers fifteen hundred years ago, than too many of our countrymen are at this day.

So they toil, and thrive, and bless God, under the glorious sun; and as for rain—they have not had rain for these two months—(I speak of April, 1864)—and, though the white limestone dust is ankle deep on every road, say that they want none for two months more, thanks, it is to be presumed, to their deep tillage, which puts the plant-roots out of the reach of drought. In spring they feed their silkworms, and wind their silk. In summer they reap their crops, and hang the maize-heads from their rafters for their own winter food, while they sell the wheat to the poor creatures, objects of their pity, who live in towns, and are forced to eat white bread. From spring to autumn they have fruit, and to spare, for themselves and for their customers; and with the autumn comes the vintage, and all its classic revelries. A happy folk—under a happy clime; which yet has its drawbacks, like all climes on earth. Terrible thunderstorms sweep over it, hail-laden, killing, battering, drowning, destroying in an hour the labours of the year; and there are ugly mistral winds likewise, of which it may be fairly said, that he who can face an eight days' mistral, without finding his life a burden, must be either a very valiant man, or have neither liver nor mucous membrane.

For on a sudden, after still and burning weather, the thermometer suddenly falls from thirty to forty degrees; and out of the north-west rushes a chilly hurricane, blowing fiercer and fiercer each day toward nightfall, and lulling in the small hours, only to burst forth again at sunrise. Parched are all lips and eyes; for the air is full of dust, yea, even of gravel which cuts like hail. Aching are all right-sides; for the sudden chill brings on all manner of liver complaints and indigestions. All who can afford it, draw tight the jalousies, and sulk in darkness; the leaves are parched, as by an Atlantic gale; the air is filled with lurid haze, as in an English north-east wind; and no man can breathe freely, or eat his bread with joy, until the plague is past.

What is the cause of these mistrals; why all the cold

K P

air of Central France should be suddenly seized with madness, and rush into the sea between the Alps and the Pyrenees ; whether the great heat of the sun, acting on the Mediterranean basin, raises up thence— as from the Gulf of Mexico—columns of warm light air, whose place has to be supplied by colder and heavier air from inland; whether the north-west mistral is, or is not, a diverted north-easter ; an arctic current which, in its right road toward the tropics across the centre of France, has been called to the eastward of the Pyrenees (instead of, as usual, to the westward), by the sudden demand for cold air,—all this let men of science decide ; and having discovered what causes the mistral, discover also what will prevent it. That would be indeed a triumph of science, and a boon to tortured humanity.

But after all, man is a worse enemy to man than any of the brute forces of nature : and a more terrible scourge than mistral or tempest swept over this land six hundred years ago, when it was, perhaps, the happiest and the most civilized portion of Europe. This was the scene of the Albigense Crusade : a tragedy of which the true history will never, perhaps, be written. It was not merely a persecution of real or supposed heretics; it was a national war, embittered by the ancient jealousies of race, between the Frank aristocracy of the north and the Gothic aristocracy of the south, who had perhaps acquired, with their half-Roman, half-Saracen civilization, mixtures both of Roman and of Saracen blood. As "Aquitanians," "Provençaux,"—Roman Provincials, as they proudly called themselves, speaking the Langue d'Oc, and looking down on the northerners who spoke the Langue d'Oïl as barbarians, they were in those days guilty of the capital crime of being foreigners ; and as foreigners they were exterminated. What their religious tenets were, we shall never know. With the Vaudois, Waldenses, "poor men of Lyons," they must not be for a moment confounded. Their creed remains to us only in the calumnies of their enemies. The confessions in the archives of the Tolosan Inquisition, as elicited either under torture or fear of torture, deserve no confidence whatsoever. And as for the licentiousness of their poetry—which has been alleged as proof of their profligacy—I can only say, that it is no more licentious than the *fabliaux* of their French conquerors, while it is far more delicate and refined. Humanity, at least, has done justice to the Troubadours of the south ; and confessed, even in the Middle Age, that to them the races of the north owed grace of expression, delicacy of sentiment, and that respect for women which soon was named chivalry ; which looks on woman, not with suspicion and contempt, but with trust and adoration ; and is not ashamed to obey her as "mistress," instead of treating her as a slave.

But these Albigenses must have had something in their hearts for which it was worth while to die. At Aviguonet, that little grey town on the crag above the railway, they burst into the place, maddened by the cruelties of the Inquisitor (an archdeacon, if I recollect rightly, from Toulouse), and slew him then and there. They were shut up in the town, and withstood heroically a long and miserable siege. At last they were starved out. The conquerors offered them their lives—so say the French stories—if they would recant. But they would not. They were thrust together into one of those stone-walled enclosures below the town, heaped over with vine-twigs and maize-stalks, and burned alive; and among them a young lady of the highest rank, who had passed through all the horrors of the siege, and was offered life, wealth, and honour, if she would turn.

Surely profligate infidels do not so die; and these poor souls, whatever were their sins or their confusions, must be numbered among the heroes of the human race.

But the world has mended since then, and so has the French character. Even before the Revolution of 1793, it was softening fast. The massacres of 1562 were not as horrible as those of the Albigense Crusade, though committed—which the former were not—under severe provocation. The massacres of 1793—in spite of all that has been said—were far less horrible than those of 1562, though they were the outpouring of centuries of pardonable fury and indignation. The crimes of the Terreur Blanche, at the Restoration—though ugly things were done in the south, especially in Nismes— were far less horrible again; though they were, for the most part, acts of direct personal retaliation on the republicans of 1793. And since then the French heart has softened fast. The irritating sense of hereditary wrong has passed away. The Frenchman conceives that justice is done to him, according to his own notions thereof. He has his share of the soil, without which no Celtic populace will ever be content. He has fair play in the battle of life; and a ' Carrière ouverte aux talens.' He has equal law and justice between man and man. And he is content; and under the sunshine of contentment and self-respect, his native good-nature expands; and he shows himself what he is, not merely a valiant and capable, but an honest, kindly, charitable man.

Yes. France has grown better, and has been growing better, I believe, for centuries past. And the difference between the France of the middle age and the France of the present day, is fitly typified by the difference between the new Carcassone below and the old Carcassone above, where every traveller, even if he be no antiquarian, should stop and gaze about a while.

The contrast is complete; and one for which a man who loves his fellow-men should surely return devout thanks to Almighty God. Below, on the west bank of the river, is the new town, spreading and growing, unwalled, for its fortifications are now replaced by boulevards and avenues; full of handsome houses; squares where, beneath the plane-tree shade, marble fountains pour out perpetual health and coolness; manufactories of gay woollens; healthy, cheerful, market folk; comfortable burghers; industry and peace. We pass outside to the great basin of the Canal de Langue-doc, and get more avenues of stately trees, and among them the red marble statue of Riquet, whose genius planned and carried out the mighty canal which joins the ocean to the sea; the wonder of its day, which proved the French to be, at least in the eighteenth cen-tury, the master-engineers of the world; the only people who still inherited the mechanical skill and daring of their Roman civilizers. Riquet bore the labour of that canal—and the calumny and obstructiveness, too, which tried to prevent its formation; France bore the expense; Louis Quatorze, of course, the glory; and no one, it is to be feared, the profit: for the navigation of the Garonne at the one extremity, and of the Mediter-ranean shallows at the other, were left unimproved till

of late years, and the canal has become practically use-
ful only just in time to be superseded by the railroads.

Now cross the Aude. Look down upon the willow
and aspen copses, where over the heads of busy
washerwomen, the nightingale and the hippolais
crowded together away from the dusty plains and
downs, shake the copses with their song; and then
toil upward to the grey fortress tower on the grey
limestone knoll; and pass, out of nature and her pure
sunshine, into the black shadow of the unnatural
Middle Age; into the region of dirt and darkness,
cruelty and fear; grim fortresses, crowded houses,
narrow streets, and pestilence. Pass through the outer
circle of walls, of the latter part of the thirteenth cen-
tury, to examine—for their architecture is a whole
history engraved in stones—the ancient walls of the
inner enceinte; massive Roman below, patched with
striped Visigothic work, with mean and hasty Moorish,
with graceful, though heavy, Romanesque of the times
of the Troubadours; a whole museum of ancient forti-
fications, which has been restored, stone by stone,
through the learning of M. Viollet le Duc and the public
spirit of the late Emperor. Pass in under the gateway,
and give yourself up to legends. There grins down on
you the broad image of the mythic Dame Carcas, who
defended the town single-handed against Charlemagne,
till this tower fell down by miracle, and let in the

Christian host. But do not believe that she **gave to** the place its name of Carcassone; for the first syllable of the word is hint enough that it was, long ere her days, a Celtic caer, or hill-fortress. Pause at the inner gate; you need not exactly believe that when the English Crusader, Simon de Montfort, burst it open, and behold, the town within was empty and desolate, he cried: 'Did I not tell you that these heretics were devils; and behold, being devils, they have vanished into air.' · You must believe, I fear, that of the great multitude who had been crowded, starving, and fever-stricken within, he found four hundred poor wretches who had lingered behind, and burnt them all alive. You need not believe that that is the mouth of the underground passage which runs all the way from the distant hills, through which the Vicomte de Beziers, after telling Simon de Montfort and the Abbot of Citeaux that he would sooner be flayed alive than betray the poor folk who had taken refuge with him, got them all safe away, men, women, and children. You need not believe that that great vaulted chamber was the 'Chamber of the Inquisition.' But you must believe that those two ugly rings let into the roof were put there for the torture of the cord; and that many a naked wretch has dangled from them ere now, confessing anything and everything that he—or, alas! she—was bidden. But these and their like are the usual furniture of every mediæval court of justice; and torture was not altogether abolished in France till the latter part of the eighteenth century. You need not believe, again, that that circular tower on the opposite side of the town was really the 'Tower of the Inquisition;' for many a feudal lord, besides the Inquisitors, had their dens of cruelty in those old times. You need not even believe—though it is too likely to be true—that that great fireplace in the little first-floor room served for the torture of the scarpines. But you must believe that in that little round den beneath it, only approached by a trap in the floor, two skeletons were found fastened by those chains to that central pillar, having died and rotted forgotten in that horrid oubliette—how many centuries ago?

'Plusieurs ont gemis là bas,' said M. Viollet le Duc's foreman of the works, as he led us out of that evil hole, to look, with eyes and hearts refreshed by the change, at a curious Visigothic tower, in which the good bishop Sidonius Apollinaris may have told of the last Burgundian invasion of his Auvergne to the good king Theodoric of the West Goths.

If anyone wishes to learn what the Middle Ages were like, let him go to Carcassone and see.

And now onward to Narbonne—or rather, to what was once Narbonne; one of the earliest colonies ever founded by the Romans; then the capital of the Visi-

gothic kingdom; then of an Arab kingdom: now a
dull fortified town—of a filth unspeakable, and not to
be forgotten or forgiven. Stay not therein an hour,
lest you take fever, or worse : but come out of the
gate over the drawbridge, and stroll down the canal.
Look back a moment, though, across the ditch. The
whole face of the wall is a museum of Roman gods,
tombs, inscriptions, bas-reliefs : the wreck of Martial's
'Pulcherrima Narbo,' the old Roman city, which was
demolished by Louis XIII., to build the ugly forti-
fications of the then new fashion, now antiquated and
useless. Take one glance, and walk on, to look at live
Nature—far more interesting than dead Art.

Everything fattens in the close damp air of the
canal. The great flat, with its heavy crops, puts you
in mind of the richest English lowland—save for the
total want of old meadows. The weeds on the bank
are English in type, only larger and richer—as be-
comes the climate. But as you look among them,
you see forms utterly new and strange, whose kinship
you cannot fancy, but which remind you that you
are nearing Italy, and Greece, and Africa. And in
the hedges are great bay-trees; and inside them,
orchards of standard fig and white mulberry, with
its long yearling shoots of glorious green—soon to
be stripped bare for the silkworms; and here and there
long lines of cypresses, black against the bright green

plain and bright blue sky. No; you are not in Britain.
Certainly not; for there is a drake (not a duck) quack-
ing with feeble treble in that cypress, six feet over
your head; and in Britain drakes do not live in trees.
You look for the climbing palmipede, and see nothing :
nor will you see; for the quacker is a tiny green tree-
frog, who holds on by the suckers at the ends of his
toes (with which he can climb a pane of glass, like a
fly), and has learnt the squirrel's art of going invisible,
without 'the receipt of fern-seed,' by simply keeping
always on the further side of the branch.

But come back; for the air even here is suggestive
of cholera and fever. The uncleanliness of these
Narbonnois is shameless and shocking; and 'immon-
dices' of every kind lie festering in the rainless heat.
The sickened botanist retreats, and buys a bottle of
Eau Bully—*alias* aromatic vinegar.

There, crowding yon hill, with handsome houses and
churches, is Beziers—the blood-stained city. Beneath
the pavement of that church, it is said, lie heaped
together the remains of thousands of men, women,
and children, slaughtered around their own altars, on
that fatal day, when the Legate Amalric, asked by
the knights how they should tell Catholics from
heretics, cried, 'Kill them all—the Lord will know
his own."

We will pass on. We have had enough of horrors. And, beside, we are longing to hurry onward; for we are nearing the Mediterranean now. There are small skiffs lying under the dark tower of Agde, another place of blood, fitly built of black lava blocks, the offspring of the nether pit. The railway cuts through rolling banks of dark lava; and now, ahead of us, is the conical lava-hill of Cette, and the mouth of the Canal du Midi.

There it is, at last. The long line of heavenly blue; and over it, far away, the white-peaked lateen sails, which we have seen in pictures since our childhood; and there, close to the rail, beyond the sand-hills, delicate wavelets are breaking for ever on a yellow beach, each in exactly the same place as the one which fell before. One glance shows us children of the Atlantic, that we are on a tideless sea.

There it is,—the sacred sea. The sea of all civilization, and almost all history, girdled by the fairest countries in the world; set there that human beings from all its shores might mingle with each other, and become humane—the sea of Egypt, of Palestine, of · Greece, of Italy, of Byzant, of Marseilles, and this Narbonnaise, 'more Roman than Rome herself,' to which we owe the greater part of our own progress; the sea, too, of Algeria and Carthage, and Cyrene, and fair lands now desolate, surely not to be desolate for ever;—the sea of civilization. Not only to the Christian, nor to the classic scholar, but to every man to whom the progress of his race from barbarism toward humanity is dear, should the Mediterranean Sea be one of the most august and precious objects on this globe; and the first sight of it should inspire reverence and delight, as of coming home—home to a rich inheritance in which he has long believed by hearsay, but which he sees at last with his own mortal corporal eyes.

Exceedingly beautiful is that first view of the sea from Cette, though altogether different in character from the views of the Mediterranean which are common in every gallery of pictures. There is nothing to remind one of Claude, or Vernet, or Stanfield. No mountain-ranges far aloft, no cliffs toppling into the water, with convents and bastides perched on their crags; and seaports, with their land-locked harbours, and quaint lighthouses, nestling on the brink. That scenery begins on the other side of the Rhone mouth, and continues, I believe, almost without interruption, to the shores of Southern Palestine, one girdle of perpetual beauty.

But here, the rail runs along a narrow strip of sand, covered with straggling vines, and tall white iris, between the sea and the great Etang de Thau, a long narrow salt-lake, beyond which the wide lowlands of

the Herault slide gently down. There is not a moun-
tain, hardly a hill, visible for miles: but all around is
the great sheet of blue glassy water: while the air is
as glassy clear as the water, and through it, at seem-
ingly immense distances, the land shows purple and
orange, blue and grey, till the landscape is one great
rainbow. White ships slide to and from far-off towns;
fishermen lounge on the marshes, drying long lines of
net. Everywhere is vastness, freedom, repose gentle
and yet not melancholy; because with all, under the
burning blue, there is that fresh wholesome heat, which
in itself is life, and youth, and joy.

Beyond, nearer the mouths of the Rhone, there are,
so men say, desolate marshes, tenanted by herds of
half-wild horses; foul mud-banks, haunted by the
pelican and the flamingo, and waders from the African
shore; a region half land, half water, where dwell
savage folk, decimated by fever and ague. But short
of those Bouches du Rhône, the railway turns to the
north, toward Montpellier and

> ' Arli, dove il Rhodano stagna.'

And at Cette ends this little tour from Ocean to Sea,
with the wish that he who next travels that way may
have as glorious weather, and as agreeable a com-
panion, as the writer of these lines had in 1864.

VI.

NORTH DEVON.

VI.

NORTH DEVON.[1]

I.—EXMOOR.

WE were riding up from Lynmouth, on a pair of ragged ponies, Claude Mellot and I, along the gorge of Watersmeet. And as we went we talked of many things; and especially of some sporting book which we had found at the Lyndale Hotel the night before, and which we had not by any means admired.[2] I do not object to sporting books in general, least of all to one on Exmoor. No place in England is more worthy of one. There is no place whose beauties and peculiarities are more likely to be thrown into strong relief by being looked at with a sportsman's eye. It is so with all forests and moorlands. The spirit of Robin Hood and Johnny of Breadislee is theirs. They are remnants of

---

[1] *Fraser's Magazine,* July 1849.

[2] Some years after this was written, the very book which was needed appeared, as "The Chase of the Red Deer," by Mr. Palk Collyns.

K   Q

the home of man's fierce youth, still consecrated to the genius of animal excitement and savage freedom; after all, not the most ignoble qualities of human nature. Besides, there is no better method of giving a living picture of a whole country than by taking some one feature of it as a guide, and bringing all other observations into harmony with that original key. Even in merely scientific books this is very possible. Look, for instance, at Hugh Miller's 'Old Red Sandstone,' 'The Voyage of the Beagle,' and Professor Forbes's work (we had almost said epic poem) on 'Glaciers.' Even an agricultural writer, if he have a real insight in him—if he have anything of that secret of the *più nel' uno,* 'the power of discovering the infinite in the finite;' of seeing, like a poet, trivial phenomena in their true relation to the whole of the great universe into which they are so cunningly fitted; if he has learned to look at all things and men, down to the meanest, as living lessons written with the finger of God; if, in short, he has any true dramatic power: then he may impart to that apparently muddiest of sciences a poetic or a humorous tone, and give the lie to Mephistopheles when he dissuades Faust from farming as an occupation too mean and filthy for a man of genius. The poetry of agriculture remains as yet, no doubt, unwritten, and the comedy of it also; though its farce-tragedy has been too often extensively enacted in practice—unconsciously to the players. As for the old 'pastoral' school, it only flourished before agriculture really existed—that is, before sound science, hard labour, and economy were necessary—and has been for the last two hundred years simply a dream. Nevertheless, as signs of what may be done even now by a genial man with so stubborn a subject as 'turnips, barley, clover, wheat,' it is worth while to look at old Arthur Young's books, both travels and treatises; and also at certain very spirited 'Chronicles of a Clay Farm,' by Talpa, which teem with humour and wisdom.

In sporting literature—a tenth muse, exclusively indigenous to England—the same observation holds good tenfold. Some of our most perfect topographical sketches have been the work of sportsmen. Old Izaak Walton, and his friend Cotton, of Dovedale, whose names will last as long as their rivers, have been followed by a long train of worthy pupils. White's 'History of Selborne;' Sir Humphry Davy's 'Salmonia;' The Wild Sports of the West;' Mr. St. John's charming little works on Highland Shooting; and, above all, Christopher North's 'Recreations'—delightful book! to be read and re-read, the tenth time even as the first —an inexhaustible fairy well, springing out of the granite rock of the sturdy Scotch heart, through the tender green turf of a genial boyish old age. Sporting books, when they are not filled—as they need never be—with low slang, and ugly sketches of ugly characters—who hang on to the skirts of the sporting world, as they would to the skirts of any other world, in default of the sporting one—form an integral and significant, and, it may be, an honourable and useful part, of the English literature of this day; and, there-fore, all shallowness, vulgarity, stupidity, or book-making in that class, must be as severely attacked as in novels and poems. We English owe too much to our field sports to allow people to talk nonsense about them.

Claude smiled at some such words of mine that day. 'You talk often of the poetry of sport. I can see nothing in it but animal excitement, and a certain quantity, I suppose, of that animal cunning which the Red Indian possesses in common with the wolf and the cat, and any other beast of prey. As a fact, the majority of sports-men are of the most unpoetical type of manhood.'

'More unpoetical than the average man of business, or man of law, Claude? Or even than the average preacher? I believe, on the contrary, that for most of them it is sport which at once keeps alive and satisfies what you would call their æsthetic faculties, and so—smile if you will—helps to make them purer, simpler, more genial men.'

'Little enough of æsthetic appears either in their conversation or their writing.'

'Esau is a dumb soul, especially here in England;

but he has as deep a heart in him as Jacob, neverthe‑
less, and as tender. Do you fancy that the gentleman
over whose book we were grumbling last night, attached
no more to his own simple words than you do ? His
account of a stag's run looks bald enough to you : but
to him (unless Diana struck him blind for intruding on
her privacy) what a whole poem of memories there
must be in those few words,—"Turned down * *
Water for a mile, and crossed the forest to Waters‑
meet, where he was run into after a gallant race." '

'A whole poem ?'

'Why not ? How can there be less, if he had eyes
to see ? '

'Does he fancy that it is an account of a run to tell
us that "Found at * * * * cover, held away at a slap‑
ping pace for * * * * Barn, then turned down the
* * * Water for a mile, and crossed the Forest ; made
for * * * Hill, but being headed, went by * * * * woods
to D * * * where he was run into after a gallant race of
* * * * hours and * * * *miles"? It is nearly as
dull as a history book ! '

'Nay, I never rode with those staghounds : and yet I
can fill up his outline for him, wherever the stag was
roused. Do you think that he never marked how the
panting cavalcade rose and fell on the huge mile‑long
waves of that vast heather sea ; how one long brown
hill after another sunk down, greyer and greyer, behind

them, and one long grey hill after another swelled up browner and browner before them; and how the sandstone rattled and flew beneath their feet, as the great horses, like Homer's of old, " devoured up the plain ;" and how they struggled down the hill-side, through bushes and rocks, and broad slipping rattling sheets of screes, and saw beneath them stag and pack galloping down the shallow glittering river-bed, throwing up the shingle, striking out the water in long glistening sheets ; and how they too swept after them, down the flat valley, rounding crag and headland, which opened one after another in interminable vista, along the narrow strip of sand and rushes, speckled with stunted, moss-bearded, heather-bedded hawthorns, between the great grim lifeless mountain walls? Did he feel no pleasant creeping of the flesh that day at the sound of his own horse-hoofs, as they swept through the long ling with a sound as soft as the brushing of a woman's tresses, and then rang down on the spongy, black, reverberating soil, chipping the honey-laden fragrant heather blossoms, and tossing them out in a rosy shower? Or, if that were really too slight a thing for the observation of an average sportsman, surely he must recollect the dying away of the hounds' voices, as the woodland passes engulfed them, whether it were Brendon or at Badgerworthy, or any other place; how they brushed through the narrow forest paths, where the ashes were already

golden, while the oaks still kept their sombre green, and
the red leaves and berries of the mountain-ash showed
bright beneath the dark forest aisles; and how all of a
sudden the wild outcry before them seemed to stop and
concentrate, thrown back, louder and louder as they
rode, off the same echoing crag; till at a sudden turn of
the road there stood the stag beneath them in the stream,
his back against the black rock with its green cushions of
dripping velvet, knee-deep in the clear amber water,
the hounds around him, some struggling and swimming
in the deep pool, some rolling and tossing and splash-
ing in a mad, half-terrified ring, as he reared into the
air on his great haunches, with the sparkling beads
running off his red mane, and dropping on his knees,
plunged his antlers down among them, with blows
which would have each brought certain death with it
if the yielding water had not broken the shock. Do
you think that he does not remember the death? The
huge carcass dragged out of the stream, followed by
dripping, panting dogs; the blowing of the mort, and the
last wild halloo, when the horn-note and the voices rang
through the autumn woods, and rolled up the smooth
flat mountain sides; and Brendon answered Countis-
bury, and Countisbury sent it on to Lynmouth hills,
till it swept out of the gorge and died away upon the
Severn sea? And then, does he not remember the
pause, and the revulsion, and the feeling of sadness

and littleness, almost of shame, as he looked up for the first time—one can pardon his not having done so before—and saw where he was, and the beauty of the hill-sides, with the lazy autumn clouds crawling about their tops, and the great sheets of screes, glaciers of stone covering acres and acres of the smooth hill-side, eating far into the woods below, bowing down the oak scrubs with their weight, and the circular sweeps of down, flecked with innumerable dark spots of gorse, each of them guarded where they open into the river chasm by two fortresses of "giant-snouted crags,"—delicate pink and grey sandstone, from which blocks and crumbling boulders have been toppling slowly down for ages, beneath the frost and the whirl-wind, and now lie in long downward streams upon the slope, as if the mountain had been weeping tears of stone? And then, as the last notes of the mort had died away, did not there come over him an awe at the silence of the woods, not broken, but deepened, by the unvarying monotone of the roaring stream beneath, which flashed and glittered, half-hidden in the dark chasm, in clear brown pools reflecting every leaf and twig, in boiling pits and walls of foam, ever changing, and yet for ever the same, fleeting on past the poor dead reeking stag and the silent hounds lying about on the moss-embroidered stones, their lolling tongues showing like bright crimson

sparkles in the deep rich Venetian air of the green
sombre shades; while the startled water-ousel, with
his white breast, flitted a few yards and stopped to
stare from a rock's point at the strange intruders;
and a single stockdove, out of the bosom of the
wood, began calling sadly and softly, with a dreamy
peaceful moan? Did he not see and hear all this, for
surely it was there to see and hear?'

'Not he. The eye only sees that which it brings
within the power of seeing; and all I shall say of him
is, that a certain apparition in white leathers was at one
period of its appearance dimly conscious of equestrian
motion towards a certain brown two-horned pheno-
menon, and other spotted phenomena, at which he had
been taught by habit to make the articulate noises
"stag" and "hounds," among certain grey, and green,
and brown phenomena, at which the same habit and
the example of his fellows had taught him to say,
"Rock, and wood, and mountain," and perhaps the
further noises of "Lovely, splendid, majestic."'

'As usual, sir! You dwellers in Babylon fancy
that you have the monopoly of all the intellect, and
all the taste, because you earn your livings by talking
about pretty things, and painting pretty things: little
do you suspect, shut up together in your little literary
worlds, and your artistic worlds, how many thousands
of us outside barbarians there are who see as clearly,

and enjoy as deeply as you do: but hold their tongues about their own feelings, simply because they have never been driven by emptiness of pocket to look round for methods of expressing them. And, after all—how much of nature can you express? You confest yourself yesterday baffled by all the magnificence around you.'

'Yes! to paint it worthily one would require to be a Turner, a Copley Fielding, and a Creswick, all in one.'

'And did you ever remark how such scenes as this gorge of the "Watersmeet" stir up a feeling of shame, almost of peevishness, before the sense of a mysterious meaning which we ought to understand and cannot?'

He smiled.

'Our torments do by length of time become our elements; and painful as that sensation is to the earnest artist, he will feel it, I fancy, at last sublime itself into an habitually gentle, reverent, almost melancholy tone of mind, as of a man bearing the burden of an infinite and wonderful message, which his own frivolity and laziness hinder him from speaking out.'

'Then it should beget in him, too, something of merciful indulgence towards the seeming stupidity of those who see, after all, only a very little shallower than he does into the unfathomable depths of nature.'

'Well, sporting books and sportsmen seem to me, by their very object, not to be worth troubling our heads about. Out of nothing, comes nothing. See, my hands are as soft as any lady's in Belgravia. I could not, to save my life, lift a hundredweight a foot off the ground; while you have been a wild man of the woods, a leaper of ditches, a rower of races, and a wanton destroyer of all animal life: and yet——'

'You would hint politely that you are as open as me to all noble, and chivalrous, and truly manly emotions?'

'What think you?'

'That you are far worthier in such matters than I, friend. But do not forget that it may be your intellect, and your profession—in one word, Heaven's mercy—which have steered you clear of shoals upon which you will find the mass of our class founder. Woe to the class or the nation which has no manly physical training! Look at the manners, the morals, the faces of the young men of the shopkeeping classes, if you wish to see the effects of utterly neglecting the physical development of man;[1] of fancying that all the muscular activity he requires under the sun is to be able to stand behind a counter, or sit on a desk-stool without tumbling off. Be sure, be sure, that ever since the days of the Persians of old, effeminacy, if not twin-sister of cowardice and dishonesty, has always gone hand in hand with them. To that utter neglect of any exer-

[1] Written before the Volunteer movement.

cises which call out fortitude, patience, self-dependence, and daring, I attribute a great deal of the low sensuality, the conceited vulgarity, the want of a high sense of honour, which is increasing just now among the middle classes; and from which the navigator, the engineer, the miner, and the sailor are comparatively free.'

'And perhaps, too, that similar want of a high sense of honour, which seems, from the religious periodicals, to pervade a large proportion of a certain more venerable profession?'

'Seriously, Claude, I believe you are not far wrong. But we are getting on delicate ground there: however, I have always found, that of whatever profession he may be—to travestie Shakspeare's words,—

> "The man that hath not sporting in his soul,
> Is fit for treason's direst stratagems"——

and so forth.'

'Civil to me!'

'Oh, you have a sporting soul in you, like hundreds of other Englishmen who never handled rod or gun; or you would not be steering for Exmoor to-day. If a lad be a genius, you may trust him to find some original means for developing his manly energies, whether in art, agriculture, science, or travels, discovery, and commerce. But if he be not, as there are a thousand chances to one he will not be, then what-

ever you teach him, let the two first things be, as they
were with the old Persians, "To speak the truth, and
to draw the bow." '

By this time we had reached the stream, just clear-
ing from the last night's showers. A long trans-
parent amber shallow, dimpled with fleeting silver
rings by rising trout; a low cascade of green-veined
snow; a deep dark pool of swirling orange-brown,
walled in with heathery rocks, and paved with sand-
stone slabs and boulders, distorted by the changing
refractions of the eddies,—sight delicious to the angler.

I commenced my sport at once, while Claude wan-
dered up the glen to sketch a knoll of crags, on which
a half-wild moorland pony, the only living thing in sight,
stood staring and snuffing at the intruder, his long
mane and tail streaming out wildly against the sky.

I had fished on for some hour or two; Claude had
long since disappeared among the hills; I fancied
myself miles from any human being, when a voice at
my elbow startled me :—

'A bleak place for fishing this, sir!'

I turned; it was an old grey-whiskered labouring
man, with pick and spade on shoulder, who had crept
on me unawares beneath the wall of the neighbouring
deer-cover. Keen honest eyes gleamed out from his
brown, scarred, weather-beaten face; and as he settled
himself against a rock with the deliberate intention of

a chat, I commenced by asking after the landlord of those parts, well known and honoured both by sportsman and by farmer.

'He was gone to Malta—a warmer place that than Exmoor.'

'What! have you been in Malta?'

Yes, he had been in Malta, and in stranger places yet. He had been a sailor: he had seen the landing in Egypt, and heard the French cannon thundering vainly from the sand-hills on the English boats. He had himself helped to lift Abercrombie up the ship's side to the death-bed of the brave. He had seen Caraccioli hanging at his own yard-arm, and heard (so he said, I know not how correctly) Lady Hamilton order out the barge herself, and row round the frigate of the murdered man, to glut her eyes with her revenge. He had seen, too, the ghastly corpse floating upright, when Nelson and the enchantress met their victim, returned from the sea-depths to stare at them, as Banquo's ghost upon Macbeth. But she was 'a mortal fine woman, was Lady Hamilton, though she was a queer one, and cruel kind to the sailors; and many a man she saved from flogging; and one from hanging, too; that was a marine that got a-stealing; for Nelson, though he was kind enough, yet it was a word and a blow with him; and quite right he, sir; for there be such rascals on board ship, that if you arn't as sharp with them as with wild beastesses, no man's life, nor the ship's neither, would be worth a day's purchase.'

So he, with his simple straightforward notions of right and wrong, worth much maudlin unmerciful indulgence which we hear in these days: and yet not going to the bottom of the matter either, as we shall see in the next war. But, rambling on, he told me how he had come home, war-worn and crippled, to marry a wife and get tall sons, and lay his bones in his native village; till which time (for death to˙the aged poor man is a Sabbath, of which he talks freely, calmly, even joyously) 'he just got his bread, by the squire's kindness, patching and mending at the stone deer-fences.'

I gave him something to buy tobacco, and watched him as he crawled away, with a sort of stunned surprise. And he had actually seen Nelson sit by Lady Hamilton! It was so strange, to have that gay Italian bay, with all its memories,—the orgies of ˌBaiæ, and the unburied wrecks of ancient towns, with the smoking crater far above; and the world-famous Nile-mouths, and those great old wars, big with the destinies of the world; and those great old heroes, with their awful deeds for good and evil, all brought so suddenly and livingly before me, up there in the desolate moorland, where the deer, and birds, and heath, and rushes were

even as they had been from the beginning. Like
Wordsworth with his Leech-Gatherer (a poem which
I, in spite of laughter, must rank among his very
highest),—

> 'While he was talking thus, the lonely place,
> The old man's shape, and speech—all troubled me:
> In my mind's eye I seemed to see him pace
> About the weary moors continually,
> Wandering about alone and silently.
> .   .   .   .   .   and when he ended,
> I could have laughed myself to scorn to find
> In that decrepit man so firm a mind.'

Just then I heard a rustle, and turning, saw Claude
toiling down to me over the hill-side. He joined me,
footsore and weary, but in great excitement; for the first
minute or two he could not speak, and at last,—

'Oh, I have seen such a sight!—but I will tell you
how it all was. After I left you I met a keeper. He
spoke civilly to me—you know my antipathy to game
and those who live thereby: but there was a wild, bold,
self-helping look about him and his gun alone there
in the waste—and after all he was a man and a brother.
Well, we fell into talk, and fraternized; and at last he
offered to take me to a neighbouring hill and show me
" sixty head of red-deer all together;" and as he spoke
he looked quite proud of his words. " I was lucky," he
said, " to come just then, for the stags had all just got
their heads again." At which speech I wondered; but

was silent, and followed him, I, Claude the Cockney, such a walk as I shall never take again. Behold these trousers—behold these hands! scratched to pieces by crawling on all-fours through the heather. But I saw them.'

'A sight worth many pairs of plaid trousers?'

'Worth Saint Chrysostom's seven years' nakedness on all-fours! And so I told the fellow, who by some cunning calculations about wind, and sun, and so forth, which he imparted to my uncomprehending ears, brought me suddenly to the top of a little crag, below which, some hundred yards off, the whole herd stood, stags, hinds—but I can't describe them. I have not brought away a scrap of sketch, though we watched them full ten minutes undiscovered; and then the stare, and the toss of those antlers, and the rush! That broke the spell with me; for I had been staring stupidly at them, trying in vain to take in the sight, with the strangest new excitement heaving and boiling up in my throat; and at the sound of their hoofs on the turf I woke, and found the keeper staring, not at them, but at me, who, I verily believe, had something very like a tear in these excitable eyes of mine.'

'"Arn't you well, sir?" said he. "You needn't be afeard; it's only at the fall of the year the stags is wicked."

'I don't know what I answered at first; but the

K   R fellow understood me when I shook his hand frantically, and told him that I should thank him to the last day of my life, and that I would not have missed it for a thousand pounds. In part-proof whereof I gave him a sovereign on the spot, which seemed to clear my character in his eyes as much as the crying at the sight of a herd of deer had mystified it.'

'Claude, well-beloved,' said I, 'will you ever speak contemptuously of sportsmen any more?'

'" Do manus," I have been vilifying them, as one does most things in the world, only for want of understanding them. How shall I do penance? Go and take service with Edwin Landseer, as pupil, colour-grinder, footboy?'

'You will then be very near to a very great poet,' quoth I, 'and one whose works will become, as centuries roll on, more and more valuable to art and to science, and, possibly, to something higher than either.'

'I begin to guess your meaning,' answered Claude.

'So we lounged, and dreamt, and fished, in heathery Highland,' as Mr. Clough would say, while the summer snipes flitted whistling up the shallow before us, and the soft, south-eastern clouds slid lazily across the sun, and the little trout snapped and dimpled at a tiny partridge hackle, with a twist of orange silk, whose elegance of shape and colour reconciled Claude's heart some-

what to my everlasting whipping of the water. When
at last :—

'You seem to have given up catching anything. You
have not stirred a fish in this last two pools, except
that little saucy yellow shrimp, who jumped over your
fly, and gave a spiteful slap at it with his tail.'

Too true; and what could be the cause? Had
that impudent sand-piper frightened all the fish on his
way up? Had an otter paralysed them with terror for
the morning? Or had a stag been down to drink?
We saw the fresh slot of his broad claws, by the bye,
in the mud a few yards back.

'We must have seen the stag himself, if he had been
here lately,' said Claude.

'Mr. Landseer knows too well by this time that that
is a non sequitur.'

'"I am no more a non sequitur than you are," an-
swered the Cornish magistrate to the barrister.'

'Fish and deer, friend, see us purblind sons of
men somewhat more quickly than we see them, fear
sharpening the senses. Perhaps, after all, the fault is
in your staring white-straw hat, a garment which has
spoilt many a good day's fishing. Ah, no! there is the
cause; the hat of a mightier than you—the thunder-
spirit himself. Thor is at hand, while the breeze, awe-
stricken, falls dead calm before his march. Behold,
climbing above that eastern ridge, his huge powdered

cauliflower-wig, barred with a grey horizontal handker-
chief of mist.'

'Oh, profane and uncomely simile!—which will next,
I presume, liken the coming hailstorm to hair-powder
shaken from the said wig.'

'To shot rather than to powder. Flee, oh, flee to
yonder pile of crags, and thank your stars that there is
one at hand; for these mountain tornadoes are at once
Tropic in their ferocity and Siberian in their cutting
cold.'

Down it came. The brown hills vanished in white
sheets of hail, first falling perpendicularly, then slanting
and driving furiously before the cold blast which issued
from the storm. The rock above us rang with the
thunder-peals; and the lightning, which might have
fallen miles away, seemed to our dazzled eyes to dive
into the glittering river at our feet. We sat silent
some half-hour, listening to the voice of One more
mighty than ourselves; and it was long after the up-
roar had rolled away among the hills, and a steady,
sighing sheet of warmer rains, from banks of low grey
fog, had succeeded the rattling of the hail upon the
crisp heather, that I turned to Claude.

'And now, since your heart is softened towards these
wild, stag-hunting, trout-fishing, jovial west-country-
men, consider whether it should not be softened like-
wise toward those old outlaw ballads which I have

never yet been able to make you admire. They express feelings not yet extinct in the minds of a large portion of the lower orders, as you would know had you lived, like me, all your life in poaching counties, and on the edges of one forest after another,—feelings which must be satisfied, even in the highest development of the civilization of the future, for they are innate in every thoughtful and energetic race,—feelings which, though they have often led to crime, have far oftener delivered from swinish sensuality ; the feelings which drove into the merry greenwood "Robin Hood, Scarlet, and John ;" "Adam Bell, and Clym of the Cleugh, and William of Cloudislee ;" the feelings which prompted one half of his inspiration to the nameless immortal who wrote the "Nutbrown Maid ;"—feelings which could not then, and cannot now, be satisfied by the drudgery of a barbaric agriculture, which, without science, economy, or enterprise, offers no food for the highest instincts of the human mind, its yearnings after Nature, after freedom, and the noble excitement of self-dependent energy.'

Our talk ended : but the rain did not : and we were at last fain to leave our shelter, and let ourselves be blown by the gale (the difficulty being not to progress forward, but to keep our feet) back to the shed where our ponies were tied, and to canter home to Lynmouth, with the rain cutting our faces like showers of pebbles, and our little mountain ponies staggering against the wind, and more than once, if Londoners will believe me, blown sheer up against the bank by some mad gust, which rushed perpendicularly, not down, but up, the chasms of the glens below.

II.—THE COAST LINE.

It is four o'clock on a May morning, and Claude and I are just embarking on board a Clovelly trawling skiff, which, having disposed of her fish at various ports along the Channel, is about to run leisurely homewards with an ebb tide, and a soft north-easterly breeze.

So farewell, fair Lynmouth; and ye storm-spirits, send us a propitious day; and dismiss those fantastic clouds which are coquetting with your thrones, crawling down one hillside, and whirling and leaping up another, in wreaths of snow, and dun, and amber, pierced every minute by some long glittering upward arrow from the rising sun, which gilds grey crags and downs a thousand feet above, while underneath the gorges still sleep black and cold in shade.

There, they have heard us! The cap rises off the 'Summer-house hill,' that eight hundred feet of upright wall, which seems ready to topple down into the nest of be-myrtled cottages at its foot; and as we sweep out into the deeper water the last mist-flake streams up from the Foreland, and vanishes in white threads into the stainless blue.

'Look at the colours of that Foreland!' cried Claude. 'The simple monotone of pearly green, broken only at intervals by blood-red stains, where the turf has slipped and left the fresh rock bare, and all glimmering softly through a delicate blue haze, like the bloom on a half-ripened plum!'

'And look, too, how the grey pebble beach is already dancing and quivering in the mirage which steams up, like the hot breath of a limekiln, from the drying stones. Talk of "glazings and scumblings," ye artists! and bungle at them as you will, what are they to Nature's own glazings, deepening every instant there behind us?'

'Mock me not. I have walked up and down here with a humbled and broken spirit, and had nearly forsworn the audacity of painting anything beyond a beech stem, or a frond of fern.'

'The little infinite in them would have baffled you just as much as the only somewhat bigger infinite of the hills on which they grow.'

'Confest: and so farewell to unpaintable Lynmouth! Farewell to the charming contrast of civilized English landscape-gardening, with its villas, and its exotics,

and its evergreens, thus strangely and yet harmo-
niously confronted with the chaos of the rocks
and mountain-streams. Those grounds of Sir William
H——'s are a double paradise, the wild Eden of the
Past side by side with the cultivated Eden of the
Future. How its alternations of Art and Savagery at
once startle and relieve the sense, as you pass sud-
denly out of wildernesses of piled boulders, and tor-
rent-shattered trees, and the roar of fern-fringed
waterfalls, into "trim walks, and fragrant alleys green;"
and the door of a summer-house transports you
at a step from Richmond to the Alps. Happy he who
"possesses," as the world calls it, and happier still he
whose taste could organize, that fairy bower.'

So he, magniloquently, as was his wont; and yet his
declamations always flowed with such a graceful ease,—
a simple, smiling earnestness,—an unpractised melody
of voice, that what would have been rant from other
lips, from his showed only as the healthy enthusiasm
of the passionate, all-seeing, all-loving artist.

'Look yonder, again,' said he, gazing up at the
huge boulder-strewn hill-side above us. 'One wonders
at that sight, whether the fable of the giants be not
true after all,—and that "Vale of Rocks," hanging five
hundred feet in air, with all its crag-castles, and totter-
ing battlements, and colossal crumbling idols, and great
blocks, which hang sloping, caught in act to fall, be not

some enormous Cyclopean temple left half-disinterred : or is it a fragment of old Chaos, left unorganized ?— or, perhaps, the waste heap of the world, where, after the rest of England had been made, some angel put up a notice for his fellows, "Dry rubbish shot here"?'

'Not so, unscientific! It is the grandfather of hills, —a fossil bone of some old continent, which stood here ages before England was. And the great earth-angel, who grinds up mountains into paint, as you do bits of ochre, for his "Continental Sketches," found in it the materials for a whole dark ground-tone of coal-measures, and a few hundred miles of warm high-lights, which we call New Red Sandstone.'

What a sea-wall they are, those Exmoor hills! Sheer upward from the sea a thousand feet rise the downs; and as we slide and stagger lazily along before the dying breeze, through the deep water which never leaves the cliff, the eye ranges, almost dizzy, up some five hundred feet of rock, dappled with every hue; from the intense dark of the tide-line, through the warm green and brown rock-shadows, out of which the horizontal cracks of the strata loom black, and the breeding gulls show like lingering snow-flakes; up to the middle cliff, where delicate grey fades into pink, pink into red, red into glowing purple; up to where the purple is streaked with glossy ivy wreaths, and black-green yews; up to where all the choir of colours vanishes abruptly on the mid-hill, to give place to one yellowish-grey sheet of upward down, sweeping aloft smooth and unbroken, except by a lonely stone, or knot of clambering sheep, and stopped by one great rounded waving line, sharp-cut against the brilliant blue. The sheep hang like white daisies upon the steep; and a solitary falcon rides, a speck in air, yet far below the crest of that tall hill. Now he sinks to the cliff edge, and hangs quivering, supported, like a kite, by the pressure of his breast and long curved wings, against the breeze.

There he hangs, the peregrine—a true 'falcon gentle,' 'sharp-notched, long-taloned, crooked-winged,' whose uncles and cousins, ages since, have struck at duck and pheasant, and sat upon the wrists of kings. And now he is full proud of any mouse or cliff-lark; like an old Chingachgook, last of the Mohicans, he lingers round 'the hunting-field of his fathers.' So all things end.

> 'The old order changeth, giving place to the new;
> And God fulfils Himself in many ways,
> Lest one good custom should corrupt the world.'

'Ay, and the day may come,' said Claude, 'when the brows of that huge High Vere shall be crowned with golden wheat, and every rock-ledge on Trentishoe, like those of Petra and the Rhine, support its garden-bed of artificial soil.'

'And when,' I answered, 'the shingly sides of that great chasm of Headon's Mouth may be clothed with the white mulberry, and the summer limestone-skiffs shall go back freighted with fabrics which vie with the finest woof of Italy and Lyons.'

'You believe, then, in the late Mrs. Whitby of Lymington?'

'Seeing is believing, Claude : through laughter, and failures, and the stupidity of half-barbarous clods, she persevered in her silk-growing, and succeeded; and I should like to put her book into the hands of every squire in Devon, Cornwall, and the South of Ireland.'

'Or require them to pass an examination in it, as one more among the many books which I intend, in my ideal kingdom, all landlords to read and digest, before they are allowed to take possession of their estates. In the meantime, what is that noble conical hill, which has increased my wonder at the infinite variety of beauty which The Spirit can produce by combinations so simple as a few grey stones and a sheet of turf?'

'The Hangman.'

'An ominous name. What is its history?

'Some sheep-stealer, they say, clambering over a wall with his booty slung round his neck, was literally hung by the poor brute's struggles, and found days after on the mountain-side, a blackened corpse on one side of the wall, with the sheep on the other, and the ravens——You may fill up the picture for yourself.'

But, see, as we round the Hangman, what a change of scene—the square - blocked sandstone cliffs dip suddenly under dark slate-beds, fantastically bent and broken by primeval earthquakes. Wooded combes, and craggy ridges of rich pasture-land, wander and slope towards a labyrinth of bush-fringed coves, black isolated tide-rocks, and land-locked harbours. There shines among the woods the Castle of Watermouth, on its lovely little salt-water loch, the safest harbour on the coast; and there is Combe-Martin, mile-long man-stye, which seven centuries of fruitless silver-mining, and of the right (now deservedly lost) of 'sending a talker to the national palaver,' have neither cleansed nor civilized. Turn, turn thy head away, dear Claude, lest even at this distance some foul odour taint the summer airs, and complete the misfortune already presaged by that pale, sad face, sickening in the burning calm! For this great sun-roasted fire-brick of the Exmoor range is fairly burning up the breeze, and we have nothing but the tide to drift us slowly down to Ilfracombe.

Now we open Rillage, and now Hillsborough, two of the most picturesque of headlands; see how their round foreheads of glistening grey shale sink down into two dark, jagged moles, running far out to sea-

ward, and tapering off, each into a long black hori-
zontal line, vanishing at last beneath its lace-fringe
of restless hissing foam. How grand the contrast of
the lightness of those sea-lines, with the solid mass
which rests upon them! Look, too, at the glaring
lights and Tartarean shadows of those chasms and
caves, which the tide never leaves, or the foot of
man explores; and listen how, at every rush of the
long ground-swell, mysterious mutterings, solemn sighs,
sudden thunders, as of a pent-up earthquake, boom
out of them across the glassy swell. Look at those
blasts of delicate vapour that shoot up from hidden
rifts, and hang a moment, and vanish; and those
green columns of wave which rush mast-high up the
perpendicular walls, and then fall back and outward
in a waterfall of foam, lacing the black rocks with a
thousand snowy streams. There they fall, and leap,
and fall again. And so they did yesterday, and the
day before; and so they did centuries ago, when the
Danes swept past them, battleworn, and sad of heart
for the loss of the magic raven flag, from the fight
at Appledore, to sit down and starve on 'the island of
Bradanrelice, which men call Flat Holms.' Ay, and
even so they leapt and fell, before a sail gleamed on the
Severn sea, when the shark and the ichthyosaur paddled
beneath the shade of tropic forests—now scanty turf
and golden gorse. And so they will leap and fall on,

on, through the centuries and the ages. O dim abyss
of Time, into which we peer shuddering, what will be
the end of thee, and of this ceaseless coil and moan of
waters ? It is true, that when thou shalt be no more,
then, too, ' there shall be no more sea ; ' and this ocean
bed, this great grave of fertility, into which all earth's
wasted riches stream, day and night, from hill and
town, shall rise and become fruitful soil, corn-field and
meadow-land ; and earth shall teem as thick with living
men as bean-fields with the summer bees ? What a
consummation ! At least there is One greater than
sea, or time : and the Judge of all the earth will do
right.

But there is Ilfracombe, with its rock-walled har-
bour, its little wood of masts within, its white terraces,
rambling up the hills, and its capstone sea-walk, the
finest ' marine parade,' as Cockneydom terms it, in all
England, except that splendid Hoe at Plymouth, ' Lam
Goemagot,' Gog-magog's leap, as the old Britains called
it, over which Corineus threw that mighty giant. And
there is the little isolated rock-chapel, where seven
hundred years ago, our west-country forefathers used
to go to pray St. Nicholas for deliverance from ship-
wreck,—a method lovingly regretted by some, as a
' pious idea of the Ages of faith.' We, however, shall
prefer the present method of lighthouses and the worthy
Trinity Board, as actually more godly and ' faithful,' as

well as more useful; and, probably, so do the sailors themselves.

But Claude is by this time nearly sick of the roasting calm, and the rolling ground-swell, and the smell of fish, and is somewhat sleepy also, between early rising and incoherent sermons; wherefore, if he takes good advice, he will stay and recruit himself at Ilfracombe, before he proceeds further with his self-elected cicerone on the grand tour of North Devon. Believe me, Claude, you will not stir from the place for a month at least. For be sure, if you are sea-sick, or heart-sick, or pocket-sick either, there is no pleasanter or cheaper place of cure (to indulge in a puff of a species now well nigh obsolete, the puff honest and true) than this same Ilfracombe, with its quiet nature and its quiet luxury, its rock fairy-land and its sea-walks, its downs and combes, its kind people, and, if possible, its still kinder climate, which combines the soft warmth of South Devon with the bracing freshness of the Welsh mountains; where winter has slipped out of the list of the seasons, and mother Earth makes up for her summer's luxury by fasting, 'not in sackcloth and ashes, but in new silk and old sack;' and instead of standing three months chin-deep in ice, and christening great snowballs her 'friends and family,' as St. Francis of Assisi did of old, knows no severer asceticism than tepid shower-baths, and a parasol of soft grey mist.

III.—MORTE.

I had been wandering over the centre of Exmoor, killing trout as I went, through a country which owes its civilization and tillage to the spirit of one man, who has found stag-preserving by no means incompatible with large agricultural improvements; among a population who still evince an unpleasant partiality for cutting and carrying farmers' crops by night, without leave or licence, and for housebreaking after the true classic method of Athens, by fairly digging holes through the house walls; a little nook of primeval savagery fast reorganizing itself under the influences of these better days. I had been on Dartmoor, too; but of that noble moorland range so much has been said and sung of late, that I really am afraid it is becoming somewhat cockney and trite. Far and wide I had wandered, rod in hand, becoming a boy again in the land of my boyhood, till, once more at Ilfracombe, opposite me sat Claude Mellot, just beginning to bloom again into cheerfulness.

We were on the point of starting for Morte, and so round to Saunton Court, and the sands beyond it; where a Clovelly trawler, which we had chartered for the occasion, had promised to send a boat on shore and take us off, provided the wind lay off the land.

But, indeed, the sea was calm as glass, the sky

cloudless azure; and the doubt was not whether we should be able to get on board through the surf, but whether, having got on board, we should not lie till nightfall, as idle

> ' As a painted ship,
> Upon a painted ocean.'

And now behold us on our way up lovely combes, with their green copses, ridges of rock, golden furze, fruit-laden orchards, and slopes of emerald pasture, pitched as steep as house-roofs, where the red long-horns are feeding, with their tails a yard above their heads; and under us, seen in bird's-eye view, the ground-plans of the little snug farms and homesteads of the Damnonii, ' dwellers in the valley,' as we West-countrymen were called of old. Now we are leaving them far below us; the blue hazy sea is showing far above the serrated ridge of the Tors, and their huge bank of sunny green : and before us is a desolate table-land of rushy pastures and mouldering banks, festooned with the delicate network of the little ivy-leaved cam-panula, loveliest of British wild-flowers, fit with its hair-like stems and tiny bells of blue to wreathe the temples of Titania. Alas ! we have passed out of the world into limbum patrum, and the region of ineffec-tuality and incompleteness. The only cultivators here, and through thousands of acres in the North of Devon, are the rook and mole : and yet the land is rich enough

K S

—the fat deep crumbling of the shale and ironstone returning year by year into the mud, from whence it hardened ages since. There are scores of farms of far worse land in mid-England, under 'a four-course shift,' yielding their load of wheat an acre. When will that land do as much? When will the spirit of Smith of Deanston and Grey of Dilston descend on North Devon? When will some true captain of industry, and Theseus of the nineteenth century, like the late Mr. Warnes of Trimmingham, teach the people here to annihilate poor-rates by growing flax upon some of the finest flax land, and in the finest flax climate, that we have in England? The shrewd Cornishmen of Launceston and Bodmin have awakened long ago to 'the new gospel of fertility.' When will North Devon awake?

'When landlords and farmers,' said Claude, 'at last acknowledge their divine vocation, and feel it a noble and heaven-ordained duty to produce food for the people of England; when they learn that to grow rushes where they might grow corn, ay, to grow four quarters of wheat where they might grow five, is to sin against God's blessings and against the English nation. No wonder that sluggards like these cry out for protection: that those who cannot take care of the land feel that they themselves need artificial care.'

'We will not talk politics, Claude. Our modern

expediency mongers have made them *pro tempore* an extinct science. "Let the dead bury their dead." The social questions are now-a-days becoming far more important than the mere House of Commons ones.'

'There does seem here and there,' he said, 'some sign of improvement. I see the paring plough at work on one field and another.'

'Swiftly goes the age, and slowly crawls improvement. The greater part of that land will be only broken up to be exhausted by corn-crop after corn-crop, till it can bear no more, and the very manure which is drawn home from it in the shape of a few turnips will be wasted by every rain of heaven, and the straw probably used to mend bad places in the road with; while the land returns to twenty years of worse sterility than ever; on the ground that—

'"Veather did zo, and gramfer did zo, and why shouldn't Jan do the zame?"' * * * *

'But here is Morte below us. "The little grey church on the windy shore," which once belonged ¹to William de Tracy, one of your friend Thomas à Becket's murderers. If you wish to vent your wrath against those who cut off your favourite Saxon hero, there is a tomb in the church which bears De Tracy's name; over which rival Dryasdusts contend fiercely with paper-arrows: the one party asserting that he became a priest, and died here in the wilderness; the others that the tomb is of later date, that he fled hence to Italy, under favour of a certain easy-going Bishop of Exeter, and died penitent and duly shriven, according to the attestations of a certain or uncertain Bishop of Cosenza.'

'Peace be with him and with the Bishop! The flight to Italy seems a very needless precaution to a man who owned this corner of the world. A bailiff would have had even less chance here then than in Connemara a hundred years ago.'

'He certainly would have fed the crabs and rock-cod in two hours after his arrival. Nevertheless, I believe the Cosenza story is the safer one.'

'What a chaos of rock-ridges!—Old starved mother Earth's bare-worn ribs and joints peeping out through every field and down; and on three sides of us, the sullen thunder of the unseen surge. What a place for some "gloom-pampered man" to sit and misanthropize!'

'"Morte," says the Devonshire proverb, "is the place on earth which heaven made last, and the devil will take first."'

'All the fitter for a misanthrope. But where are the trees? I have not seen one for the last four miles.'

'Nor will you for a few miles more. Whatever will grow here (and most things will) they will not, except, at least, hereafter the sea-pine of the Biscay shore. You would know why, if you had ever felt a south-westerly gale here, when the foam-flakes are flying miles inland, and you are fain to cling breathless to bank and bush, if you want to get one look at those black fields of shark's-tooth tide-rocks, champing and churning the great green rollers into snow. Wild folk are these here, gatherers of shell-fish and laver, and merciless to wrecked vessels, which they consider as their own by immemorial usage, or rather right divine. Significant, how an agricultural people is generally as cruel to wrecked seamen, as a fishing one is merciful. I could tell you twenty stories of the baysmen down there to the westward risking themselves like very heroes to save strangers' lives, and beating off the labouring folk who swarmed down for plunder from the inland hills.'

'Knowledge, you see, breeds sympathy and love. But what a merciless coast!'

'Hardly a winter passes without a wreck or two. You see there lying about the timbers of more than one tall ship. You see, too, that black rock a-wash far out at sea, apparently a submarine outlier of the north horn of this wide rock-amphitheatre below us. That is the Morte stone, the "Death-rock," as the Normans christened it of old; and it does not belie its name even now. See how, even in this calm, it hurls up its column of spray at every wave; and then conceive being entrapped between it and the cliffs, on some blinding, whirling winter's night, when the land is shrouded thick in clouds, and the roar of the breakers hardly precedes by a minute the crash of your bows against the rocks.'

'I never think, on principle, of things so painful, and yet so irrelievable. Yet why does not your much-admired Trinity House erect a light there?'

'So ask the sailors; for it is indeed one of the gate-way-jambs of the Channel, and the deep water and the line of coast tempt all craft to pass as close to it as possible.'

'Look at that sheet of yellow sand below us now, banked to the inland with sand-hills and sunny downs, and ending abruptly at the foot of that sombre wall of slate-hill, which runs out like a huge pier into the sea some two miles off.'

'That is Woollacombe: but here on our right is a sight worth seeing. Every gully and creek there among the rocks is yellow, but not with sand. Those are shells; the sweepings of the ocean bed for miles around, piled there, millions upon millions, yards deep, in every stage of destruction. There they lie grinding to dust; and every gale brings in fresh myriads from the inexhaustible sea-world, as if Death could be never tired of devouring, or God of making. The brain grows dizzy and tired, as one's feet crunch over the endless variety of their forms.'

'And then one recollects that every one of them has been a living thing—a whole history of birth, and growth, and propagation, and death. Waste it cannot be, or cruelty on the part of the Maker: but why this infinite development of life, apparently only to furnish out of it now and then a cartload of shell-sand to these lazy farmers? But after all, there is not so much life in all those shells put together as in one little child: and it may die the hour that it is born! What we call life is but an appearance and a becoming; the true life of existence belongs only to spirits. And whether or not we, or the sea-shell there, are at any given moment helping to make up part of some pretty little pattern in this great kaleidoscope called the material universe, yet, in the spirit all live to Him, and shall do so for ever.'

And thereon he rambled off into a long lecture on 'species-spirits,' and 'individual-spirits,' and 'personal spirits,' doubtless most important. But I, what between the sun, the luncheon, and the metaphysic, sank into soft slumbers, from which I was only awakened by the carriage stopping, according to our order, on the top of Saunton hill.

We left the fly, and wandered down towards the old gabled court, nestling amid huge walnuts in its south-

ward glen; while before us spread a panorama, half
sea, half land, than which, perhaps, our England owns
few lovelier.

At our feet was a sea of sand—for the half-mile to
the right smooth as a floor, bounded by a broad band
of curling waves, which crept slowly shorewards with
the advancing tide. Right underneath us the sand
was drifted for miles into fantastic hills, which quivered
in the heat, the glaring yellow of its lights chequered
by delicate pink shadows and sheets of grey-green bent.
To the left were rich alluvial marshes, covered with red
cattle sleeping in the sun, and laced with creeks and
flowery dykes; and here and there a scarlet line, which
gladdened Claude's eye as being a 'bit of positive
colour in the foreground,' and mine, because they were
draining tiles. Beyond again, two broad tide-rivers,
spotted with white and red-brown sails, gleamed like
avenues of silver, past knots of gay dwellings, and tall
lighthouses, and church-towers, and wandered each on
its own road, till they vanished among the wooded
hills. On the eastern horizon the dark range of Exmoor
sank gradually into lower and more broken ridges,
which rolled away, woodland beyond woodland, till
all outlines were lost in purple haze; while, far
beyond, the granite peaks of Dartmoor hung like a
delicate blue cloud, and enticed the eye away into
infinity. From hence, as our eyes swept round the

horizon, the broken hills above the river's mouth gradually rose into the table-land of the 'barren coal-measures' some ten miles off,—a long straight wall of cliffs which bounded the broad bay, buried in deepest shadow, except where the opening of some glen revealed far depths of sunlit wood. A faint perpendicular line of white houses, midway along the range, marked our destination; and far to the westward, the land ended sheer and suddenly at the cliffs of Hartland, the 'Promontory of Hercules,' as the old Romans called it, to reappear some ten miles out in the Atlantic, in the blue flat-topped island of Lundy, so exactly similar in height and form to the opposite cape, that it required no scientific imagination to supply the vast gap which the primæval currents had sawn out. There it all lay beneath us like a map; its thousand hues toned down harmoniously into each other by the summer haze, and 'the eye was not filled with seeing,' nor the spirit with the intoxicating sight of infinitely various life and form in perfectest repose.

I was the first to break the silence.

'Claude, well-beloved, will you not sketch a little?'
No answer.

'Not even rhapsodize? call it "lovely, exquisite, grand, majestic"? There are plenty of such words in worldlings' mouths—not a Cockney but would burst out with some enthusiastic commonplace at such a sight—surely one or other of them must be appropriate.'

'Silence, profane! and take me away from this. Let us go down, and hide our stupidities among those sand-hills, and so forget the whole. What use standing here to be maddened by this tantalizing earth-spirit, who shows us such glorious things, and will not tell us what they mean?'

So down we went upon the burrows, among the sands, which hid from us every object but their own chaotic curves and mounds. Above, a hundred skylarks made the air ring with carollings; strange and gaudy plants flecked the waste round us; and insects without number whirred over our heads, or hung poised with their wings outspread on the tall stalks of marram grass. All at once a cloud hid the sun, and a summer whirlwind, presage of the thunderstorm, swept past us, carrying up with it a column of dry sand, and rattling the dry bents over our heads.

'What a chill, doleful sigh comes from those reeds!' said Claude. 'I can conceive this desert, beneath a driving winter's sky instead of this burning azure, one of the most desolate places on the earth.'

'Ay, desolate enough,' I said, as we walked down beyond the tide-mark, over the vast fields of ribbed and splashy sands, 'when the dead shells are rolling and crawling up the beach in wreaths before the gale,

with a ghastly rattle as of the dry bones in the " Valley
of Vision," and when not a flower shows on that sand-
cliff, which is now one broad bed of yellow, scarlet, and
azure.'

'That is the first spot in England,' said Claude,
'except, of course, "the meads of golden king-cups,"
where I have seen wild flowers give a tone to the
colouring of the whole landscape, as they are said to do
in the prairies of Texas. And look how flowers
and cliff are both glowing in a warm green haze, like
that of Cuyp's wonderful sandcliff picture in the Dul-
wich Gallery,—wonderful, as I think, and true, let
some critics revile it as much as they will.'

'Strange, that you should have quoted that picture
here; its curious resemblance to this very place first
awoke in me, years ago, a living interest in landscape-
painting. But look there; even in these grand summer
days there is a sight before us sad enough. There are
the ribs of some ill-fated ship, a man-of-war too, as
the story goes, standing like black fangs, half-buried
in the sand. And off what are those two ravens
rising, stirring up with their obscene wings a sickly,
putrescent odour? A corpse?'

No, it was not a corpse; but the token of many
corpses. A fragment of some ship; its gay green
paint and half-effaced gilding contrasting mockingly
with the long ugly feathered barnacle-shells, which

clustered on it, rotting into slime beneath the sun, and torn and scattered by the greedy beaks of the ravens.

In what tropic tornado, or on what coral-key of the Bahamas, months ago, to judge by those barnacles, had that tall ship gone down? How long had that scrap of wreck gone wandering down the Gulf Stream, from Newfoundland into the Mid-Atlantic, and hitherward on its homeless voyage toward the Spitzbergen shore? And who were all those living men who "went down to Hades, even many stalwart souls of heroes," to give no sign until the sea shall render up her dead? And every one of them had a father and mother—a wife, perhaps, and children, waiting for him—at least a whole human life, childhood, boyhood, manhood, in him. All those years of toil and education, to get him so far on his life-voyage; and here is the end thereof!'

'Say rather, the beginning thereof,' Claude answered, stepping into the boat. 'This wreck is but a torn scrap of the chrysalis-cocoon; we may meet the butterflies themselves hereafter.'

*   *   *   *   *

And now we are on board; and alas! some time before the breeze will be so. Take care of that huge boom, landsman Claude, swaying and sweeping backwards and forwards across the deck, unless you wish to be knocked overboard. Take care, too, of that loose rope's end, unless you wish to have your eyes cut out. Take my advice, lie down here across the deck, as others are doing. Cover yourself with great-coats, like an Irishman, to keep yourself cool, and let us meditate a little on this strange thing, and strange place, which holds us now.

Look at those spars, how they creak and groan with every heave of the long glassy swell. How those sails flap, and thunder, and rage, with useless outcries and struggles—only because they are idle. Let the wind take them, and they will be steady, silent in an instant—their deafening dissonant grumbling exchanged for the soft victorious song of the breeze through the rigging, musical, self-contented, as of bird on bough. So it is through life; there is no true rest but labour. "No true misery," as Carlyle says, "but in that of not being able to work." Some may call it a pretty conceit. I call it a great world-wide law, which reaches from earth to heaven. Whatever the Preacher may have thought it in a moment of despondency, what is it but a blessing that "sun, and wind, and rivers, and ocean," as he says, and "all things, are full of labour—man cannot utter it." This sea which bears us would rot and poison, did it not sweep in and out here twice a day in swift refreshing current; nay, more, in the very water which laps

against our bows troops of negro girls may have
hunted the purblind shark in West Indian harbours,
beneath glaring white-walled towns, with their rows
of green jalousies, and cocoa-nuts, and shaddock groves.
For on those white sands there to the left, year by
year, are washed up foreign canes, cassia beans, and
tropic seeds ; and sometimes, too, the tropic ocean
snails, with their fragile shells of amethystine blue,
come floating in mysteriously in fleets from the far
west out of the passing Gulf Stream, where they have
been sailing out their little life, never touching shore
or ground, but buoyed each by his cluster of air-bubbles,
pumped in at will under the skin of his tiny foot, by
some cunning machinery of valves—small creatures
truly, but very wonderful to men who have learned
to reverence not merely the size of things, but the
wisdom of their idea, and raising strange longings and
dreams about that submarine ocean-world which
stretches, teeming with richer life than this terrestrial
one, away, away there westward, down the path of
the sun, toward the future centre of the world's
destiny.

Wonderful ocean-world ! three-fifths of our planet !
Can it be true that no rational beings are denizens
there ? Science is severely silent—having as yet seen
no mermaids : our captain there forward is not silent—
if he has not seen them, plenty of his friends have.

The young man here has been just telling me that it was only last month one followed a West Indiaman right across the Atlantic. "For," says he, "there must be mermaids, and such like. Do you think Heaven would have made all that water there only for the herrings and mackerel?"

I do not know, Tom : but I, too, suspect not; and I do know that honest men's guesses are sometimes found by science to have been prophecies, and that there is no smoke without fire, and few universal legends without their nucleus of fact. After all, those sea-ladies are too lovely a dream to part with in a hurry, at the mere despotic fiat of stern old Dame Analysis, divine and reverend as she is. Why, like Keats's Lamia,

'Must all charms flee,
At the mere touch of cold Philosophy,'

who will not even condescend to be awe-struck at the new wonders which she herself reveals daily? Perhaps, too, according to the Duke of Wellington's great dictum, that each man must be the best judge in his own profession, sailors may know best whether mermaids exist or not. Besides, was it not here on Croyde Sands abreast of us, this very last summer, that a maiden— by which beautiful old word West-country people still call young girls—was followed up the shore by a mermaid who issued from the breakers, green-haired, golden-combed, and all; and, fleeing home, took to her bed and died, poor thing, of sheer terror in the course of a few days, persisting in her account of the monster? True, the mermaid may have been an overgrown Lundy Island seal, carried out of his usual haunts by spring-tides and a school of fish. Be it so. Lundy and its seals are wonderful enough in all reason to thinking men, as it looms up there out of the Atlantic, with its two great square headlands, not twenty miles from us, in the white summer haze. We will go there some day, and pick up a wild tale or two about it.

But, lo! a black line creeps up the western horizon. Tom, gesticulating, swears that he sees 'a billow break.' True: there they come; the great white horses, that 'champ and chafe, and toss in the spray.' That long-becalmed trawler to seaward fills, and heels over, and begins to tug and leap impatiently at the weight of her heavy trawl. Five minutes more, and the breeze will be down upon us. The young men whistle openly to woo it; the old father thinks such a superstition somewhat beneath both his years and his religion, but cannot help pursing up his lips into a sly 'whe-eugh' when he has got well forward out of sight.

*   *   *   *   *

Five long minutes; there is a breath of air; a soft distant murmur; the white horses curve their necks,

and dive and vanish; and rise again like snowy por-
poises, nearer, and nearer, and nearer. Father and
sons are struggling with that raving, riotous, drunken
squaresail forward; while we haul away upon the
main-sheet.

When will it come? It is dying back—sliding past
us. 'Hope deferred maketh the heart sick.' No,
louder and nearer swells 'the voice of many waters,'
'the countless laugh of ocean,' like the mirth of ten
thousand girls, before us, behind us, round us; and
the oily swell darkens into crisp velvet-green, till the
air strikes us, and heels us over; and leaping, plunging,
thrashing our bows into the seas, we spring away close-
hauled upon the ever-freshening breeze, while Claude is
holding on by ropes and bulwarks, and some, whose
sea-legs have not yet forgot their craft, are swinging
like a pendulum as they pace the deck, enjoying, as the
Norse vikings would have called it, 'the gallop of the
flying sea-horse, and the shiver of her tawny wings.'

Exquisite motion! more maddening than the smooth
floating stride of the race-horse, or the crash of the
thorn-hedges before the stalwart hunter, or the swaying
of the fir-boughs in the gale, when we used to climb as
schoolboys after the lofty hawk's nest; but not so
maddening as the new motion of our age—the rush
of the express-train, when the live iron pants and
leaps and roars through the long chalk cutting; and

K   T

white mounds gleam cold a moment against the sky and vanish; and rocks, and grass, and bushes, fleet by in dim blended lines; and the long hedges revolve like the spokes of a gigantic wheel; and far below, meadows, and streams, and homesteads, with all their lazy old-world life, open for an instant, and then flee away; while awe-struck, silent, choked with the mingled sense of pride and helplessness, we are swept on by that great pulse of England's life-blood, rushing down her iron veins; and dimly out of the future looms the fulfilment of our primæval mission, to conquer and subdue the earth, and space too, and time, and all things,—even, hardest of all tasks, yourselves, my cunning brothers; ever learning some fresh lesson, except that hardest one of all, that it is the Spirit of God which giveth you understanding.

Yes, great railroads, and great railroad age, who would exchange you, with all your sins, for any other time? For swiftly as rushes matter, more swiftly rushes mind; more swiftly still rushes the heavenly dawn up the eastern sky. 'The night is far spent, the day is at hand.' 'Blessed is that servant whom his Lord, when He cometh, shall find watching!'

But come, my poor Claude, I see you are too sick for such deep subjects; so let us while away the time by picking the brains of this tall handsome boy at the helm, who is humming a love-song to himself sotto

voce, lest it should be overheard by the grey-headed
father, who is forward, poring over his Wesleyan hymn-
book. He will have something to tell you; he has a
soul in him looking out of those wild dark eyes, and
delicate aquiline features of his. He is no spade-
drudge or bullet-headed Saxon clod: he has in his veins
the blood of Danish rovers and passionate southern
Milesians, who came hither from Teffrobani, the Isle
of Summer, as the old Fenic myths inform us. Come
and chat with him. You dare not stir? Perhaps you
are in the right. I shall go and fraternize, and bring
you reports.   *   *   *   *

He has been, at all events, 'up the Straits' as
the Mediterranean voyage is called here, and seen
'Palermy' and the Sicilians. But, for his imagination,
what seems to have struck it most was that it was a
'fine place for Jack, for a man could get mools there
for a matter of three-halfpence a-day.'

'And was that all you got out of him?' asked Claude,
sickly and sulkily.

'Oh, you must not forget the halo of glory and
excitement which in a sailor's eyes surrounds the de-
lights of horseback. But he gave me besides a long
glowing account of the catechism which they had there,
three-quarters of a mile long.'

'Pope Pius's catechism, I suppose?'

So thought I, at first; but it appeared that all the

dead of the city were arranged therein, dried and dressed out in their finest clothes, 'every sect and age,' as Tom said, 'by itself, as natural as life!' We may hence opine that he means some catacombs or other.

Poor Claude could not even get up a smile : but his sorrows were coming swiftly to an end. The rock clefts grew sharper and sharper before us. The soft masses of the lofty bank of wooded cliff rose higher and higher. The white houses of Clovelly, piled stair above stair up the rocks, gleamed more and more brightly out of the green round bosoms of the forest. As we shut in headland after headland, one tall conical rock after another darkened with its black pyramid the bright orb of the setting sun. Soon we began to hear the soft murmur of the snowy surf line ; then the merry voices of the children along the shore ; and running straight for the cliff-foot, we slipped into the little pier, from whence the red-sailed herring-boats were swarming forth like bees out of a hive, full of gay handsome faces, and all the busy blue-jacketed life of seaport towns, to their night's fishing in the bay.

IV.—CLOVELLY.

A couple of days had passed, and I was crawling up the paved stairs inaccessible to cart or carriage, which are flatteringly denominated 'Clovelly-street,' a

landing-net full of shells in one hand, and a couple of
mackerel lines in the other; behind me a sheer descent,
roof below roof, at an angle of 45°, to the pier and
bay, 200 feet below, and in front, another hundred
feet above, a green amphitheatre of oak, and ash,
and larch, shutting out all but a narrow slip of sky,
across which the low, soft, formless mist was crawling,
opening every instant to show some gap of intense
dark rainy blue, and send down a hot vaporous gleam
of sunshine upon the white cottages, with their grey
steaming roofs, and bright green railings, packed one
above another upon the ledges of the cliff; and on the
tall tree-fuchsias and gaudy dahlias in the little scraps
of court-yard, calling the rich faint odour out of the
verbenas and jessamines, and, alas! out of the herring-
heads and tails also, as they lay in the rivulet; and
lighting up the wings of the gorgeous butterflies, almost
unknown in our colder eastern climate, which fluttered
from woodland down to garden, and from garden up
to woodland, and seemed to form the connecting link
between that swarming hive of human industry and
the deep wild woods in which it was embosomed. So up
I was crawling, to dine off gurnards of my own catching,
—excellent fish, despised by deluded Cockneys, who
fancy that because its head is large and prickly, therefore
its flesh is not as firm, and sweet, and white, as that
of any cod who ever gobbled shell-fish,—when down

the stair front of me, greasy as ice from the daily
shower, came slipping and staggering, my friend
Claude, armed with camp-stool and portfolio.

'Where have you been wandering to-day?' I asked.
'Have you yet been as far as the park, which, as I
told you, would supply such endless subjects for your
pencil?'

'Not I. I have been roaming up and down this
same "New Road" above us; and find there materials
for a good week's more work, if I could afford it.
Indeed, it was only to-day, for the first time, that I
got as far as the lodge at the end of it, and then was
glad enough to turn back shuddering at the first
glimpse of the flat, dreary moorland beyond,—as Adam
may have turned back into Eden after a peep out of
the gates of Paradise.'

He should have taken courage and gone a half-
mile further,—to the furze-grown ruins of a great
Roman camp, which gives its name to the place, 'Clo-
velly,'—Vallum Clausum, or Vallis Clausa, as anti-
quarians derive it; perhaps, 'the hidden camp,' or
glen,—perhaps something else. Who cares? The old
Romans were there, at least 10,000 strong: and some
sentimental tribune or other of them had taste enough
to perch his summer-house out on a conical point of
the Hartland Cliffs, now tumbling into the sea, tes-
selated pavement, baths and all. And strange work,

no doubt, went on in that lonely nook, looking out
over the Atlantic swell,—nights and days fit for Petro-
nius's own pen, among a seraglio of dark Celtic beauties.
Perhaps it could not be otherwise. An ugly state of
things—as heathen conquests always must have been ;
yet even in it there was a use and meaning. But
they are past like a dream, those 10,000 stalwart
men, who looked far and wide over the Damnonian
moors from a station which would be, even in these
days, a first-rate military position. Gone, too, are the
old Saxon Franklins who succeeded. Old Wrengils,
or some such name, whoever he was, at last found
some one's bill too hard for his brain-pan; and there
he lies on the hill above, in his ' barrow ' of Wrinkle-
bury. And gone, too, the gay Norman squire, who, as
tradition says, kept his fair lady in the old watch-
tower, on the highest point of the White Cliff—' Gal-
lantry Bower,' as they call it to this day—now a mere
ring of turf-covered stones, and a few low stunted oaks,
shorn by the Atlantic blasts into the shape of two huge
cannon, which form a favourite landmark for the fisher-
men of the bay. Gone they all are, Cymry and Roman,
Saxon and Norman ; and upon the ruins of their ac-
cumulated labour we stand here. Each of them had
his use,—planted a few more trees or cleared a few
more, tilled a fresh scrap of down, organized a scrap
more of chaos. Who dare wish the tide of improve-

ment, which has been flowing for nineteen centuries, swifter and swifter still as it goes on, to stop, just because it is not convenient to us just now to move on? It will not take another nineteen hundred years, be sure, to make even this lovely nook as superior to what it is now as it is now to the little knot of fishing huts where naked Britons peeped out, trembling at the iron tramp of each insolent legionary from the camp above. It will not take another nineteen hundred years to develope the capabilities of this place,—to make it the finest fishery in England, next to Torbay, —the only safe harbour of refuge for West Indiamen, along sixty miles of ruthless coast,—and a commercial centre for a vast tract of half-tilled land within, which only requires means of conveyance to be as fertile and valuable as nine-tenths of England. Meanwhile Claude ought to have seen the deer-park. The panorama from that old ruined ' bower ' of cliff and woodland, down and sea, is really unique in its way.

' So is the whole place, in my eyes,' said Claude. ' I have seen nothing in England to be compared to this little strip of paradise between two great waste worlds of sea and moor. Lynmouth might be matched among the mountains of Wales and Ireland. The first three miles of the Rheidol, from the Devil's Bridge towards Aberystwith, or the gorge of the Wye, down the opposite watershed of the same mountains, from Castle

Dufferin down to Rhaiadyr, are equal to it in mag-
nificence of form and colour, and superior in size.
But I question whether anything ever charmed me
more than did the return to the sounds of nature
which greeted me to-day, as I turned back from the
dreary, silent moorland turnpike into this new road,
terraced along the cliffs and woods—those who first
thought of cutting it must have had souls in them
above the herd—and listened to a glorious concert in
four parts, blending and supporting each other in
exquisite harmony, from the shrill treble of a thousand
birds, and the soft melancholy alto of the moaning
woods, downward through the rich tenor hum of
innumerable insects, who hung like sparks of fire
beneath the glades of oak, to the bass of the unseen
surge below,

> "Whose deep and dreadful organ-pipe,"

far below me, contrasted strangely with the rich soft
inland character of the deep woods, luxuriant ferns,
and gaudy flowers. It is that very contrast which
makes the place so unique. One is accustomed to
connect with the notion of the sea bare cliffs, breezy
downs, stunted shrubs struggling for existence : and
instead of them behold a forest wall, 500 feet high, of
almost semi-tropic luxuriance. At one turn, a deep
glen, with its sea of green woods, filled up at the mouth

with the bright azure sheet of ocean.—Then some long
stretch of the road would be banked on one side with
crumbling rocks, festooned with heath, and golden
hawkweed, and London pride, like velvet cushions
covered with pink lace, and beds of white bramble
blossom alive with butterflies; while above my head,
and on my right, the cool canopy of oak and
birch leaves shrouded me so close, that I could have
fancied myself miles inland, buried in some glen un-
known to any wind of heaven, but that everywhere
between green sprays and grey stems, gleamed that
same boundless ocean blue, seeming, from the height
at which I was, to mount into the very sky. It looked
but a step out of the leafy covert into blank infinity.
And then, as the road wound round some point, one's
eye could fall down, down, through the abyss of per-
pendicular wood, tree below tree clinging to and clothing
the cliff, or rather no cliff, but perpendicular sheet of
deep wood sedge, and broad crown ferns, spreading
their circular fans.—But there is no describing them,
or painting them either.—And then to see how the
midday sunbeams leapt past one down the abyss,
throwing out here a grey stem by one point of bur-
nished silver, there a hazel branch by a single leaf of
glowing golden green, shooting long bright arrows
down, through the dim, hot, hazy atmosphere of the
wood, till it rested at last upon the dappled beach

of pink and grey pebbles, and the dappled surge which wandered up and down among them, and broke up into richer intricacy with its chequer-work of woodland shadows, the restless net of snowy foam.'

'You must be fresh from reading Mr. Ruskin's book, Claude, to be able to give birth to such a piece of complex magniloquence as that last period of yours.'

'Why, I saw all that, and ten thousand things more; and yet do you complain of me for having tried to put one out of all those thousand things into words? And what do you mean by sneering at Mr. Ruskin? Are there not in his books more and finer passages of descriptive poetry—word-painting—call them what you will, than in any other prose book in the English language?'

'Not a doubt of it, my dear Claude; but it will not do for every one to try Mr. Ruskin's tools. Neither you nor I possess that almost Roman severity, that stern precision of conception and expression, which enables him to revel in the most gorgeous language, without ever letting it pall upon the reader's taste by affectation or over-lusciousness. His style is like the very hills along which you have been travelling, whose woods enrich, without enervating, the grand simplicity of their forms.'

'The comparison is just,' said Claude. 'Mr. Ruskin's style, like those very hills, and like, too, the Norman cathedrals of which he is so fond, is rather magnified than concealed by the innumerable multiplicity of its ornamental chasing and colouring.'

'And is not that,' I asked, 'the very highest achievement of artistic style?'

'Doubtless. The severe and grand simplicity, of which folks talk so much, is great indeed; but only the greatest as long as men are still ignorant of Nature's art of draping her forms with colour, chiaroscuro, ornament, not at the expense of the original design, but in order to perfect it by making it appeal to every faculty instead of those of form and size alone.'

'Still you will allow the beauty of a bare rock, a down, a church spire, a sheet or line of horizontal water,—their necessity to the completion of a landscape. I recollect well having the value of a stern straight line in Nature brought home to me, when, during a long ride in the New Forest, after my eye had become quite dulled and wearied with the monotonous softness of rolling lawns, feathery heath, and rounded oak and beech woods, I suddenly caught sight of the sharp peaked roof of Rhinefield Lodge, and its row of tall stiff poplar-spires, cutting the endless sea of curves. The relief to my eye was delicious. I really believe it heightened the pleasure with which I reined in my mare for a chat with old Toomer the keeper, and the noble bloodhound who eyed me from between his master's legs.'

'I can well believe it. Simple lines in a landscape are of the same value as the naked parts of a richly-clothed figure. They act both as contrasts and as indications of the original substratum of the figure; but to say that severe simplicity is the highest ideal is mere pedantry and Manicheism.'

'Oh, everything is Manicheism with you, Claude!'

'And no wonder, while the world is as full of it now as it was in the thirteenth century. But let that pass. This craving after so-called classic art, whether it be Manicheism or not, is certainly a fighting against God, —a contempt of everything which He has taught us artists since the introduction of Christianity. I abominate this setting up of Sculpture above Painting, of the Greeks above the Italians,—as if all Eastern civilization, all Christian truth, had taught art nothing,—as if there was not more real beauty in a French cathedral or a Venetian palazzo than in a dozen Parthenons, and more soul in one Rafaelle, or Titian either, than in all the Greek statues of the Tribune or Vatican.'

'You have changed your creed, I see, and, like all converts, are somewhat fierce and fanatical. You used to believe in Zeuxis and Parrhasius in old times.'

'Yes, as long as I believed in Fuseli's "Lectures;" but when I saw at Pompeii the ancient paintings which still remain to us, my faith in their powers received its first shock; and when I re-read in the Lectures of

Fuseli and his school all their extravagant praises of the Greek painters, and separated their few facts fairly out from among the floods of rant on which they floated, I came to the conclusion that the ancients knew as little of colour or chiaroscuro as they did of perspective, and as little of spiritual expression as they did of land-scape-painting. What do I care for the birds pecking at Zeuxis's grapes, or Zeuxis himself trying to draw back Parrhasius's curtain? Imitative art is the lowest trickery. There are twenty men in England now capable of the same sleight of hand; and yet these are recorded as the very highest triumphs of ancient art by the only men who have handed down to us any record of it.'

'It may be so; or again, it may not. But do not fancy, Claude, that classic sculpture has finished its work on earth. You know that it has taught you what Gothic art could never teach,—the ideal of physical health and strength. Believe that it exists, and will exist, to remind the puny town-dweller of the existence of that ideal; to say to the artisan, every time he looks upon a statue—such God intended you to be; such you may be; such your class will be, in some future healthy state of civilization, when Sanitary Reform and Social Science shall be accepted and carried out as primary duties of a government toward the nation.

'Surely, classic sculpture remains, as a witness of the primæval paradise; a witness that man and woman were created at first healthy, and strong, and fair, and innocent; just as classic literature remains for a witness that the heathen of old were taught of God; that we have something to learn of them, summed up in that now obsolete word "virtue"—true and wholesome manhood, which we are likely to forget, and are forgetting daily, under the enervating shadow of popular superstitions.[1] And till we have learnt that, may Greek books still form the basis of our liberal education, and may Greek statues, or even English attempts to copy them, fill public halls and private houses. This generation may not understand their divine and eternal significance; but a future generation, doubt it not, will spell it out right well.'

Claude and I went forth along the cliffs of a park, which, though not of the largest, is certainly of the loveliest in England,—perhaps unique, from that abrupt contact of the richest inland scenery with the open sea, which is its distinctive feature. As we wandered along the edge of the cliff, beneath us on our left lay wooded valleys, lawns spotted with deer, stately timber trees, oak and beech, birch and alder, growing as full

---

[1] Most wise and noble words upon this matter, worth the attention of all thinking men, and above all of clergymen, have been written by Mr. J. S. Mill, in his tract on 'Liberty.'

and round-headed as if they had been buried in some Shropshire valley fifty miles inland, instead of having the Atlantic breezes all the winter long sweeping past a few hundred feet above their still seclusion. Glens of forest wound away into the high inner land, with silver burns sparkling here and there under their deep shadows; while from the lawns beneath, the ground sloped rapidly upwards towards us, to stop short in a sheer wall of cliff, over which the deer were leaning to crop the shoots of ivy, where the slipping of a stone would have sent them 400 feet perpendicular into the sea. On our right, from our very feet, the sea spread out to the horizon; a single falcon was wheeling about the ledges below; a single cormorant was fishing in the breakers, diving and rising again like some tiny water-beetle;

> ‘ The murmuring surge
> That on the unnumbered pebbles idly chafed
> Could not be heard so high.’

The only sound beside the rustle of the fern before the startled deer was the soft mysterious treble of the wind as it swept over the face of the cliff beneath us; but the cool air was confined to the hill-tops round; beneath, from within a short distance of the shore, the sea was shrouded in soft summer haze. The far Atlantic lay like an ocean of white wool, out of which the Hart-land Cliffs and the highest point of Lundy just showed their black peaks. Here and there the western sun caught one white bank of mist after another, and tinged them with glowing gold; while nearer us long silvery zigzag tide-lines, which we could have fancied the tracks of water-fairies, wandered away under the smoky grey-brown shadows of the fog, and seemed to vanish hundreds of miles off into the void of space, so completely was all notion of size or distance destroyed by the soft gradations of the mist. Suddenly, as we stood watching, a breeze from the eastward dived into the basin of the bay, swept the clouds out, packed them together, rolled them over each other, and hurled them into the air miles high in one Cordillera of snowy mountains, sailing slowly out into the Atlantic; and behold, instead of the chaos of mist, the whole amphitheatre of cliffs, with their gay green woods and spots of bright red marl and cold black ironstone, and the gleaming white sands of Braunton, and the hills of Exmoor bathed in sunshine, so near and clear we almost fancied we could see the pink heather-hue upon them; and the bay one vast rainbow, ten miles of flame-colour and purple, emerald and ultramarine, flecked with a thousand spots of flying snow. No one knows what gigantic effects of colour even our temperate zone can show, till they have been in Devonshire and Cornwall; and last, but not least, in Ireland— the Emerald Isle, in truth. No stay-at-home knows

K   U

the colour of the sea till he has seen the West of England; and no one, either stay-at-home or traveller, I suspect, knows what the colour of a green field can be till he has seen it among the magic smiles and tears of an Irish summer shower in county Down.

Down we wandered from our height through 'trim walks and alleys green,' where the arbutus and gum-cistus fringed the cliffs, and through the deep glades of the park, towards the delicious little cove which bounds it.—A deep crack in the wooded hills, an old mill half buried in rocks and flowers, a stream tinkling on from one rock-basin to another towards the beach, a sandy lawn gay with sea-side flowers over which wild boys and bare-footed girls were driving their ponies with panniers full of sand, and as they rattled back to the beach for a fresh load, standing upright on the backs of their steeds, with one foot in each pannier, at full trot over rocks and stones where a landsman would find it difficult to walk on his own legs.

Enraptured with the place and people, Claude pulled out his sketch-book and sat down.

'What extraordinary rocks!' said he, at length. 'How different from those Cyclopean blocks and walls along the Exmoor cliffs are these rich purple and olive ironstone layers, with their sharp serrated lines and polished slabs, set up on edge, snapped, bent double, twisted into serpentine curves, every sheet of cliff scored with sharp parallel lines at some fresh fantastic angle!'

Yes; there must have been strange work here when all these strata were being pressed and squeezed together like a ream of wet paper between the rival granite pincers of Dartmoor and Lundy. They must have suffered enough then in a few years to give them a fair right to lie quiet till Doomsday, as they seem likely to do. But it is only old Mother Earth who has fallen asleep hereabouts. Air and sea are just as live as ever. Ay, lovely and calm enough spread beneath us there the broad semicircle of the bay; but to know what it can be, it should be seen as I have seen it, when, in the roaring December morning, we have been galloping along the cliffs, wreck-hunting.—One morning I can remember well, how we watched from the Hartland Cliffs a great barque, which came drifting and rolling in before the western gale, while we followed her up the coast, parsons and sportsmen, farmers and Preventive men, with the Manby's mortar lumbering behind us in a cart, through stone gaps and track-ways, from headland to headland.—The maddening excitement of expectation as she ran wildly towards the cliffs at our feet, and then sheered off again inexplicably;—her foremast and bowsprit, I recollect, were gone short off by the deck; a few rags of sail fluttered from her

main and mizen. But with all straining of eyes and
glasses, we could discern no sign of man on board.
Well I recollect the mingled disappointment and admi-
ration of the Preventive men, as a fresh set of salvors
appeared in view, in the form of a boat's crew of Clovelly
fishermen; how we watched breathlessly the little black
speck crawling and struggling up in the teeth of the
gale, under the shelter of the land, till, when the ship
had rounded a point into smoother water, she seized on
her like some tiny spider on a huge unwieldy fly; and
then how one still smaller black speck showed aloft on
the main-yard, and another—and then the desperate
efforts to get the topsail set—and how we saw it tear
out of their hands again, and again, and again, and
almost fancied we could hear the thunder of its flap-
pings above the roar of the gale, and the mountains
of surf which made the rocks ring beneath our feet;—
and how we stood silent, shuddering, expecting every
moment to see whirled into the sea from the plunging
yards one of those same tiny black specks, in each one
of which was a living human soul, with sad women
praying for him at home! And then how they tried to
get her head round to the wind, and disappeared in-
stantly in a cloud of white spray—and let her head
fall back again—and jammed it round again, and dis-
appeared again—and at last let her drive helplessly up
the bay, while we kept pace with her along the cliffs;

and how at last, when she had been mastered and fairly
taken in tow, and was within two miles of the pier,
and all hearts were merry with the hopes of a prize
which would make them rich, perhaps, for years to
come—one-third, I suppose, of the whole value of her
cargo—how she broke loose from them at the last
moment, and rushed frantically in upon those huge
rocks below us, leaping great banks of slate at the blow
of each breaker, tearing off masses of ironstone which
lie there to this day to tell the tale, till she drove
up high and dry against the cliff, and lay, like an
enormous stranded whale, grinding and crashing her-
self to pieces against the walls of her adamantine cage.
And well I recollect the sad records of the log-book
which was left on board the deserted ship; how she had
been waterlogged for weeks and weeks, buoyed up by
her timber cargo, the crew clinging in the tops, and
crawling down, when they dared, for putrid biscuit-
dust and drops of water, till the water was washed
overboard and gone; and then notice after notice, 'On
this day such an one died,' 'On this day such an one
was washed away'—the log kept up to the last, even
when there was only that to tell, by the stern busi-
ness-like merchant skipper, whoever he was; and how
at last, when there was neither food nor water, the
strong man's heart seemed to have quailed, or perhaps
risen, into a prayer, jotted down in the log—'The Lord

have mercy on us!'—and then a blank of several pages, and, scribbled with a famine-shaken hand, 'Remember thy Creator in the days of thy youth;'—and so the log and the ship were left to the rats, which covered the deck when our men boarded her. And well I remember the last act of that tragedy; for a ship has really, as sailors feel, a personality, almost a life and soul of her own; and as long as her timbers hold together, all is not over. You can hardly call her a corpse, though the human beings who inhabited her, and were her soul, may have fled into the far eternities; and so we felt that night, as we came down along the woodland road, with the north-west wind hurling dead branches and showers of crisp oak-leaves about our heads; till suddenly, as we staggered out of the wood, we came upon such a piece of chiaroscuro as would have baffled Correggio, or Rembrandt himself. Under a wall was a long tent of sails and spars, filled with Preventive men, fishermen, Lloyd's underwriters, lying about in every variety of strange attitude and costume; while candles, stuck in bayonet-handles in the wall, poured out a wild glare over shaggy faces and glittering weapons, and piles of timber, and rusty iron cable, that glowed red-hot in the light, and then streamed up the glen towards us through the salt misty air in long fans of light, sending fiery bars over the brown transparent oak foliage and the sad beds of withered autumn flowers, and glorifying the wild flakes of foam, as they rushed across the light-stream, into troops of tiny silver angels, that vanished into the night and hid them-selves among the woods from the fierce spirit of the storm. And then, just where the glare of the lights and watch-fires was most brilliant, there too the black shadows of the cliff had placed the point of intensest darkness, lightening gradually upwards right and left, between the two great jaws of the glen, into a chaos of grey mist, where the eye could discern no form of sea or cloud, but a perpetual shifting and quivering as if the whole atmosphere was writhing with agony in the clutches of the wind.

The ship was breaking up; and we sat by her like hopeless physicians by a deathbed-side, to watch the last struggle,—and 'the effects of the deceased.' I recollect our literally warping ourselves down to the beach, holding on by rocks and posts. There was a saddened awe-struck silence, even upon the gentleman from Lloyd's with the pen behind his ear. A sudden turn of the clouds let in a wild gleam of moonshine upon the white leaping heads of the breakers, and on the pyramid of the Black-church Rock, which stands in summer in such calm grandeur gazing down on the smiling bay, with the white sand of Braunton and the red cliffs of Portledge shining through its two vast arches; and against a slab of rock on the right, for years afterwards discoloured with her paint, lay the ship, rising slowly on every surge, to drop again with a piteous crash as the wave fell back from the cliff, and dragged the roaring pebbles back with it under the coming wall of foam. You have heard of ships at the last moment crying aloud like living things in agony ? I heard it then, as the stumps of her masts rocked and reeled in her, and every plank and joint strained and screamed with the dreadful tension.

A horrible image—a human being shrieking on the rack, rose up before me at those strange semi-human cries, and would not be put away—and I tried to turn, and yet my eyes were riveted on the black mass, which seemed vainly to implore the help of man against the stern ministers of the Omnipotent.

Still she seemed to linger in the death-struggle, and we turned at last away; when, lo ! a wave, huger than all before it, rushed up the boulders towards us.—We had just time to save ourselves.—A dull, thunderous groan, as if a mountain had collapsed, rose above the roar of the tempest; and we all turned with an instinctive knowledge of what had happened, just in time to see the huge mass melt away into the boiling white, and vanish for evermore. And then the very raving of the wind seemed hushed with awe ; the very breakers plunged more silently towards the shore, with something of a sullen compunction; and as we stood and strained our eyes into the gloom, one black plank after another crawled up out of the darkness upon the head of the coming surge, and threw itself at our feet like the corpse of a drowning man, too spent to struggle more.

There is another subject for a picture for you, my friend Claude: but your gayer fancy will prefer the scene just as you are sketching it now, as still and bright as if this coast had never seen the bay darkened with the grey columns of the waterspouts, stalking across the waves before the northern gale; and the tiny herring-boats fleeing from their nets right for the breakers, hoping more mercy even from those iron walls of rock than from the pitiless howling waste of spray behind them; and that merry beach beside the town covered with shrieking women and old men casting themselves on the pebbles in fruitless agonies of prayer, as corpse after corpse swept up at the feet of wife and child, till in one case alone a single dawn saw upwards of sixty widows and orphans weeping over those who had gone out the night before in the fulness of strength and courage. Hardly an old playmate of mine, but is drowned and gone :—

> 'Their graves are scattered far and wide
> By mount, by stream, and sea.'

One poor little fellow's face starts out of the depths

of memory as fresh as ever, my especial pet and bird-
nesting companion as a boy—a little delicate, precocious,
large-brained child, who might have written books
some day, if he had been a gentleman's son : but when
his father's ship was wrecked, they found him, left alone
of all the crew, just as he had been lashed into the
rigging by loving and dying hands, but cold and stiff,
the little soul beaten out of him by the cruel waves
before it had time to show what growth there might
have been in it. We will talk no more of such things.
It is thankless to be sad when all heaven and earth are
keeping holiday under the smile of God.

'And now let us return. At four o'clock to-morrow
morning, you know, we are to start for Lundy.'

V.—LUNDY.

It was four o'clock on an August morning. Our
little party had made the sleeping streets ring with jests
and greetings, as it collected on the pier. Some dozen
young men and women, sons and daughters of the
wealthier coasting captains and owners of fishing-
smacks, chaperoned by our old landlord, whose delicate
and gentlemanlike features and figure were strangely at
variance with the history of his life,—daring smuggler,
daring man-of-war sailor, and then most daring and
successful of coastguard-men. After years of fighting

and shipwreck and creeping for kegs of brandy; after having seen, too—sight not to be forgotten—the Walcheren dykes and the Walcheren fever, through weary months of pestilence, he had come back with a little fortune of prize-money to be a village oracle, loving and beloved, as gentle and courteous as if he had never 'stato al inferno,' and looked Death in the face. Heaven bless thee, shrewd loyal heart, a gentleman of God's making, not unrecognized either by many of men's making.

The other chaperone was a lady of God's making, too; one who might have been a St. Theresa, had she been born there and then; but as it was, had been fated to become only the Wesleyan abbess of the town, and, like Deborah, 'a mother in Israel.' With her tall, slim, queenly figure, massive forehead, glittering eyes, features beaming with tenderness and enthusiasm, and yet overcast with a peculiar expression of self-consciousness and restraint, well known to those who have studied the physiognomies of 'saints,' she seemed to want only the dress of some monastic order to make her the ideal of a mediæval abbess, watching with a half-pitying, half-complacent smile, the gambols of a group of innocent young worldlings. I saw Claude gazing at her full of admiration and surprise, which latter was certainly not decreased when, as soon as all had settled themselves comfortably on board, and the cutter was slipping quietly away under the magnificent deer-park cliffs, the Lady Abbess, pulling out her Wesleyan hymn-book, gave out the Morning Hymn, apparently as a matter of course.

With hardly a demur one sweet voice after another arose; then a man gained courage, and chimed in with a full harmonious bass; then a rich sad alto made itself heard, as it wandered in and out between the voices of the men and women; and at last a wild mellow tenor, which we discovered after much searching to proceed from the most unlikely-looking lips of an old dry, weather-bleared, mummified chrysalis of a man, who stood aft, steering with his legs, and showing no sign of life except when he slowly and solemnly filled his nose with snuff.

'What strange people have you brought me among?' asked Claude. 'I have been wondering ever since I came here at the splendid faces and figures of men, women, and children, which popped out upon me from every door in that human rabbit-burrow above. I have been in raptures at the gracefulness, the courtesy, the intelligence of almost everyone I meet; and now, to crown all, everyone among them seems to be a musician.'

'Really you are not far wrong, and you will find them as remarkable morally as they are physically and intellectually. The simplicity and purity of the women here put one more in mind of the valleys of the Tyrol than of an English village.'

'And in proportion to their purity, I suppose,' said Claude, 'is their freedom and affectionateness?'

'Exactly. It would do your "naturalist" heart good, Claude, to see a young fellow just landed from a foreign voyage rolling up the street which we have just descended, and availing himself of the immemorial right belonging to such cases of kissing and being kissed by every woman whom he meets, young and old. You will find yourself here among those who are too simple-minded, and too full of self-respect, to be either servile or uncourteous.'

'I have found out already that Liberty, Fraternity, and Equality, in such company as this, are infinitely pleasanter, as well as cheaper, than the aristocratic seclusion of a cutter hired for our own behoof.'

'True; and now you will not go home and, as most tourists do, say that you know a place, without knowing the people who live in it—as if the human inhabitants of a range of scenery were not among its integral and most important parts——'

'What! are Copley Fielding's South Down landscapes incomplete without a half-starved seven shillings a-week labourer in the foreground?'

'Honestly, are they not a text without a sermon? a premise without a conclusion? Is it not partly

because the land is down, and not well-tilled arable,
that the labourer is what he is? And yet, perhaps,
the very absence of human beings in his vast sheets of
landscape, when one considers that they are scraps of
great, overcrowded, scientific England in the nineteenth
century, is in itself the bitterest of satires. But, hush!
there is another hymn commencing—not to be the last
by many.'

*　　　*　　　*　　　*　　　*

We had landed, and laughed, and scrambled, eaten
and drunk, seen all the sights of Lundy, and heard all
the traditions. Are they not written in Mr. Bamfield's
Ilfracombe Guide? Why has not some one already
written a fire-and-brimstone romance about them?
'Moresco Castle; or, the Pirate Knight of the Atlantic
Wave.' What a title! Or again—'The Seal Fiend; or,
the Nemesis of the Scuttled West Indiaman.'—If I had
paper and lubricité enough, and that delightful careless-
ness of any moral or purpose, except that of fine writing
and money-making, which possesses some modern
scribblers—I could tales unfold—— But neither pirate
legends, nor tales of cheated insurance offices, nor
wrecks and murders, will make us understand Lundy—
what it is 'considered in its idea,' as the new argot
is. It may be defined as a lighthouse-bearing island.
The whole three miles of granite table-land, seals, sea-
birds, and human beings, are mere accidents and ap-

pendages—the pedestal and the ornaments of that
great white tower in the centre, whose sleepless fiery
eye blinks all night long over the night-mists of the
Atlantic. If, as a wise man has said, the days will come
when our degenerate posterity will fall down and wor-
ship rusty locomotives and fossil electric-telegraphs, the
relics of their ancestors' science, grown to them mythic
and impossible, as the Easter-islanders bow before the
colossal statues left by a nobler and extinct race, then
surely there will be pilgrimages to Lundy, and prayers
to that white granite tower, with its unglazed lantern
and rusting machinery, to light itself up again, and
help poor human beings! Really, my dear brothers, I
am not in jest : you seem but too likely now-a-days
to arrive at some such catastrophe—sentimental philo-
sophy for the 'enlightened' few, and fetish-worship
(of which nominally Christian forms are as possible
as heathen ones) for the masses.—At that you may
only too probably arrive—unless you repent, and 'get
back your souls.'

*   *   *   *   *

We had shot along the cliffs a red-legged chough
or two, and one of the real black English rat, exter-
minated on the mainland by the grey Hanoverian new-
comer; and weary with sight-seeing and scrambling, we
sat down to meditate on a slab of granite, which hung
three hundred feet in air above the western main.

'This is even more strange and new to me,' said Claude, at length, 'than anything I have yet seen in this lovely West. I now appreciate Ruskin's advice to oil-painters to go and study the coasts of Devon and Cornwall, instead of lingering about the muddy seas and tame cliffs of the Channel and the German Ocean.'

'How clear and brilliant,' said I, ' everything shows through this Atlantic atmosphere. The intensity of colouring may vie with that of the shores of the Mediterranean. The very raininess of the climate, by condensing the moisture into an ever-changing phantasmagoria of clouds, leaves the clear air and sunshine, when we do get a glimpse of them, all the more pure and transparent.'

'The distinctive feature of the scene is, in my eyes, the daring juxtaposition of large simple masses of positive colour. There are none of the misty enamelled tones of Lynmouth, or the luscious richness of Clovelly. The forms are so simple and severe, that they would be absolutely meagre, were it not for the rich colouring with which Nature has so lovingly made up for the absence of all softness, all picturesque outline. One does not regret or even feel the want of trees here, while the eye ranges down from that dappled cloud-world above, over that sheet of purple heather, those dells bedded with dark green fern, of a depth and richness of hue which I never saw before

—over those bright grey granite rocks, spangled with black glittering mica and golden lichens, to rest at last on that sea below, which streams past the island in a swift roaring torrent of tide.'

'Sea, Claude? say, ocean. This is real Atlantic blue here beneath us. No more Severn mud, no more grass-green bay-water, but real ocean sapphire—dark, deep, intense, Homeric purple, it spreads away, away, there before us, without a break or islet, to the shores of America. You are sitting on one of the last points of Europe; and therefore all things round you are stern and strange with a barbaric pomp, such as befits the boundary of a world.'

'Ay, the very form of the cliffs shows them to be the breakwaters of a continent. No more fantastic curves and bands of slate, such as harmonize so well with the fairyland which we left this morning; the cliffs, with their horizontal rows of cubical blocks, seem built up by Cyclopean hands.'

'Yet how symbolic is the difference between them and that equally Cyclopic masonry of the Exmoor coast. There every fracture is fresh, sharp-edged, crystalline; the worn-out useless hills are dropping to pieces with their own weight. Here each cube is delicately rounded off at the edges, every crack worn out into a sinuous furrow, like the scars of an everlasting warfare with the winds and waves.'

K   X

'Does it not raise strange longings in you,' said Claude, 'to gaze out yonder over the infinite calm, and then to remember that beyond it lies America!—the new world; the future world; the great Titan-baby, who will be teeming with new Athens and Londons, with new Bacons and Shakspeares, Newtons and Goethes, when this old worn-out island will be—what? Oh! when I look out here, like a bird from its cage, a captive from his dungeon, and remember what lies behind me, to what I must return to-morrow—the over-peopled Babylon of misery and misrule, puffery and covetousness—and there before me great countries untilled, uncivilized, unchristianized, crying aloud for man to come and be man indeed, and replenish the earth and subdue it. "Oh that I had wings as a dove, then would I flee away and be at rest!" Here, lead me away; my body is growing as dizzy as my mind. I feel coming over me that horrible longing of which I have heard, to leap out into empty space. How the blank air whispers, "Be free!" How the broad sea smiles, and calls, with its ten thousand waves, "Be free!"—As I live, if you do not take me away I shall throw myself over the cliff.'

I did take him away, for I knew the sensation and its danger well. It has nothing to do with physical giddiness. Those who are cliff-bred, and who never were giddy for an instant in their lives, have often felt themselves impelled to leap from masts, and tree-tops, and cliffs; and nothing but the most violent effort of will could break the fascination. I cannot but think, by the bye, that many a puzzling suicide might be traced to this same emotion acting on a weak and morbid brain.

We returned to the little landing cove. The red-sailed cutter lay sleeping below us—'floating double, ship and shadow.' Shoals of innumerable mackerel broke up, making acres of water foam and sparkle round their silvery sides, with a soft roar (call it 'a bull' if you like, it is the only expression for that mysterious sound), while among them the black head of a huge seal was slowly and silently appearing and vanishing, as he got his dinner, in a quiet business-like way, among the unhappy wanderers.

We put off in the boat, and just halfway from the cutter Claude gave a start, and the women a scream, as the enormous brute quietly raised his head and shoulders out of the water ten yards off, with a fish kicking in his mouth, and the water running off his nose, to take a deliberate stare at us, after the fashion of seals, whose ruling passion is curiosity. The sound of a musical instrument, the sight of a man bathing—anything, in short, which their small wits cannot explain at first sight, is enough to make them forget all their cunning, and thrust their heads suicidally into any danger; and even so it fared with the 'black man,' as the girls, in their first terror, declared him to be. Some fellow's gun went off—of itself I should like to believe—but the whole charge disappeared into his sleek round visage, knocking the mackerel from between his teeth; and he turned over, a seven-foot lump of lifeless blubber.

'Wretch!' cried Claude, as we dragged the seal into the boat, where he lay with his head and arms hanging helplessly over the bows, like a sea-sick alderman on board a Margate steamer. 'What excuse can he give for such a piece of wanton cruelty?'

'I assure you his skin and oil are very valuable.'

'Pish!—Was he thinking of skin and oil when he pulled the trigger? or merely obeying the fleshly lust of destructiveness—the puppet of two bumps on the back of his head?'

'My dear Claude, man is the microcosm; and as the highest animal, the ideal type of the mammalia, he, like all true types, comprises in himself the attributes of all lower species. Therefore he must have a tiger-vein in him, my dear Claude, as well as a beaver-vein and a spider-vein; and no more shame to him. You are a butterfly; that good fellow a beast of prey; both may have their own work to do in this age just as they had in the old ones; and if you do not like that explanation, all I can say is, I can sympathise with you and

with him too. Homo sum—humani nihil a me alienum
puto. Trim the boat, lads, or the seal will swamp us,
and, like Samson, slay more in his death than ever he
slew in his life.'

We slipped on homeward. The cliff-wall of Lundy
stood out blacker and blacker every moment against
the gay western sky; greens, greys, and purples, dyeing
together into one deep rich monotone, for which our
narrow colour-vocabulary has no word; and threw a
long cold shadow towards us across the golden sea;
suddenly above its dark ridge a wild wreath of low
rack caught the rays of the setting sun, and flamed up
like a volcano towards the dun and purple canopy of
upper clouds. Before us the blue sea and the blue
land-line were fading into mournful grey, on which one
huge West Indiaman blazed out, orange and scarlet, her
crowded canvas all a-flame from the truck to the water's
edge.—A few moments and she, too, had vanished into
the grey twilight, and a chill night-wind crisped the
sea. It was a relief to hear the Evening Hymn rise
rich and full from one voice, and then another and
another, till the men chimed in one by one, and the
whole cutter, from stem to stern, breathed up its
melody into the silent night.

But the hymn soon flagged—there was more mirth
on board than could vent itself in old Charles Wesley's
words; and one began to hum a song tune, and then

another, with a side glance at the expression of the
Lady Abbess's face, till at last, when a fair wife took
courage, and burst out with full pipe into 'The sea,
the sea,' the ice was fairly broken; and among jests
and laughter one merry harmless song after another
rang out, many of them, to Claude's surprise, fashion-
able London ones, which sounded strangely enough out
there on the wild western sea.   At last—

'Claude, friend,' I whispered, 'you must sing your
share too—and mine also, for that matter.'

'What shall I sing?'

'Anything you will, from the sublime to the ridi-
culous.   They will understand and appreciate it as well
as yourself. Recollect, you are not among bullet-headed
South Saxon clods, but among wits as keen and imagi-
nations as rich as those of any Scotch shepherd or
Manchester operative.'

And up rose his exquisite tenor.

This was his first song, but it was not allowed to be
his last.   German ballads, Italian Opera airs, were all
just as warmly, and perhaps far more sincerely ap-
preciated, as they would have been by any London
evening-party; and the singing went on, hour after
hour, as we slipped slowly on upon the tide, till it
grew late, and the sweet voices died away one by one;
and then the Liberty, Equality, and Fraternity which
had reigned so pleasantly throughout the day took a

new form, as the women huddled together to sleep in each other's arms; and the men and we clustered forwards, while from every mouth fragrant incense steamed upwards into the air. 'Man a cooking animal?' my dear Doctor Johnson—pooh! man is a smoking animal. There is his ergon, his 'differential energy,' as the Aristotelians say—his true distinction from the ourang-outang. Ponder it well.

The men were leaning on the trawl capstan, while our old landlord, with half-a-dozen pipes within a foot of his face, droned out some long sea-yarn about Ostend, and muds, and snow-storms, and revenue-cruisers going down stern foremost, kegs of brandy and French prisons, which I shall not repeat; for indeed the public has been surfeited with sea-stories of late, from many sufficiently dull ones up to the genial wisdom of 'Peter Simple,' and the gorgeous word-painting of 'Tom Cringle's Log.' And now the subject is stale—the old war and the wonders thereof have died away into the past, like the men who fought in it; and Trafalgar and the Bellerophon are replaced by Manchester and 'Mary Barton.' We have solved the old sea-going problems pretty well—thanks to wise English-hearted Captain Marryat, now gone to his rest, just when his work was done; and we must turn round and face a few land-going problems not quite so easy of solution. So Claude and I thought, as we leant over the sloop's

bows, listening neither to the Ostend story forwards
nor the forty-stanza ballad aft, which the old steersman
was moaning on, careless of listeners, to keep himself
awake at the helm.　Forty stanzas or so we did count
from curiosity; the first line of each of which ended
infallibly with

'Says the commodo—ore;

and the third with

'Says the female smuggler;'

and then gave up in despair; and watched in a dreamy,
tired, half-sad mood, the everlasting sparkle of the
water as our bows threw it gently off in sheets of flame
and 'tender curving lines of creamy' fire, that ran
along the glassy surface, and seemed to awaken the sea
for yards round into glittering life, as countless dia-
monds, and emeralds, and topazes, leaped and ran and
dived round us, while we slipped slowly by; and then a
speck of light would show far off in the blank darkness,
and another, and another, and slide slowly up to us—
shoals of medusæ, every one of them a heaving globe of
flame; and some unseen guillemot would give a startled
squeak, or a shearwater close above our heads suddenly
stopped the yarn, and raised a titter among the men,
by his ridiculously articulate, and not over-compli-
mentary, cry; and then a fox's bark from the cliffs
came wild and shrill, although so faint and distant;

or the lazy gaff gave a sad uneasy creak; and then a
soft warm air, laden with heather honey, and fragrant
odours of sedge, and birch, and oak, came sighing from
the land; while all around us was the dense blank of
the night, except where now and then some lonely
gleam through the southern clouds showed the cliff-
tops on our right.—It was all most unearthly, dream-
like, a strange phantasmagoria, like some scene from
'The Ancient Mariner'—all the world shut out, silent,
invisible, and we floating along there alone, like a fairy
ship creeping through Chaos and the unknown Limbo.
Was it an evil thought that rose within me as I said to
Claude—

'Is not this too like life? Our only light the
sparkles that rise up round us at every step, and die
behind us; and all around, and all before, the great
black unfathomable eternities? A few souls brought
together as it were by chance, for a short friendship
and mutual dependence in this little ship of earth, so
soon to land her passengers and break up the company
for ever?'

He smiled.

'There is a devil's meaning to everything in nature,
and a God's meaning, too. Your friends, the zoolo-
gists, have surely taught you better than that. As I
read Nature's parable to-night, I find nothing in it but
hope. What if there be darkness, the sun will rise to-

morrow. What if there seem a chaos : the great organic world is still living, and growing, and feeding, unseen by us, all the black night through; and every phosphoric atom there below is a sign that even in the darkest night there is still the power of light, ready to flash out, wherever and however it is stirred. Does the age seem to you dark ? Do you, too, feel as I do at times, the awful sadness of that text,—"The time shall come when ye shall desire to see one of the days of the Lord, and shall not see it"? Then remember that

" The night is never so long
But at last it ringeth for matin song."

And even as it is around us here, so it is in the world of men. The night is peopled not merely with phantoms and wizards, superstitions and spirits of evil, but under its shadow all sciences, methods, social energies, are taking rest, and growing, and feeding, unknown to themselves, that they may awake into a new life, and intermarry, and beget children nobler than themselves, when "the day-spring from on high comes down." Even now, see ! the dawn is gilding the highest souls, as it is those Exmoor peaks afar; and we are in the night only because we crawl below. What if we be unconscious of all the living energies which are fermenting round us now ? Have you not shown me in this last week every moorland pool, every drop of the summer sea, alive with beautiful organizations, multiplying as fast as the thoughts of man? Is not every leaf breathing still, every sap vein drinking still, though we may not see them? "Even so is the kingdom of God; like seed sown in the ground; and men rise, and lie down and sleep; and it groweth up they know not how."'

We both fell into a reverie. The story and the ballad were finished, and not a sound broke the silence except the screaming of the sea-fowl, which led my thoughts wandering back to nights long past, when we dragged the seine up to our chins in water through the short midsummer night, and scrambled and rolled over on the beach in boyish glee, after the skate and mullet, with those now gone; and as I thought and thought, old voices seemed to call me, old faces looked at me, of playmates, and those nearer than playmates, now sleeping in the deep deep sea, amid far coral islands; and old figures seemed to glide out of the mysterious dark along the still sea floor, as if the ocean were indeed giving up her dead. I shook myself, turned away, and tried to persuade myself that I was dreaming. Perhaps I had been doing so. At least, I remember very little more, till I was roused by the rattling of the chain-cable through the hawse-hole, opposite the pier-head.

And now, gentle readers, farewell; and farewell,

Clovelly, and all the loving hearts it holds; and fare-well, too, the soft still summer weather. Claude and I are taking our last walk together along the deer-park cliffs. Lundy is shrouded in the great grey fan of dappled haze which streams up from the westward, dimming the sickly sun. 'There is not a breath the blue wave to curl.' Yet lo! round Chapman's Head creeps a huge bank of polished swell, and bursts in thunder on the cliffs.—Another follows, and another.—The Atlantic gales are sending in their avant-courriers of ground-swell: six hours more, and the storm which has been sweeping over 'the still-vexed Bermoöthes,' and bending the tall palms on West Indian isles, will be roaring through the oak woods of Devon. The old black buck is calling his does with ominous croakings, and leading the way slowly into the deepest coverts of the glens. The stormy petrels, driven in from the Atlantic, are skimming like black swallows over the bay beneath us. Long strings of sea-fowl are flagging on steadily at rail-road pace, towards the sands and salt-marshes of Braunton. The herring-boats are hastily hauling their nets—you may see the fish sparkling like flakes of silver as they come up over the gunwale; all craft, large and small, are making for the shelter of the pier. Claude starts this afternoon to sit for six months in Babylonic smoke, working up his sketches into certain unspeakable pictures, with which the world will be astonished, or otherwise, at the next Royal Academy Exhibition; while I, for whom another fortnight of pure western air remains, am off to well-known streams, to be in time for the autumn floods, and the shoals of fresh-run salmon trout.

THE END.

LONDON :

R. CLAY, SONS, AND TAYLOR, PRINTERS,

BREAD STREET HILL,